Think/Make

Think/Make

Della Valle Bernheimer

Andrew Bernheimer and Jared Della Valle

Princeton Architectural Press
New York

//

Graham Foundation / Princeton Architectural Press series
New Voices in Architecture
presents first monographs on emerging designers from around the world

Published by
Princeton Architectural Press
37 East Seventh Street
New York, New York 10003

For a free catalog of books, call 1.800.722.6657.
Visit our website at www.papress.com.

Editor: Laurie Manfra
Designer: Jan Haux

Special thanks to: Nettie Aljian, Bree Anne Apperley, Sara Bader,
Nicola Bednarek, Janet Behning, Becca Casbon, Carina Cha,
Penny (Yuen Pik) Chu, Carolyn Deuschle, Russell Fernandez,
Pete Fitzpatrick, Wendy Fuller, Clare Jacobson, Aileen Kwun,
Nancy Eklund Later, Linda Lee, John Myers, Katharine Myers,
Lauren Nelson Packard, Dan Simon, Andrew Stepanian,
Jennifer Thompson, Paul Wagner, Joseph Weston, and Deb Wood
of Princeton Architectural Press
—Kevin C. Lippert, publisher

Library of Congress Cataloging-in-Publication Data
Bernheimer, Andrew, 1968–
Think/make : Della Valle Bernheimer / Andrew Bernheimer and Jared
Della Valle. — 1st ed.
p. cm. — (New voices in architecture)
Includes bibliographical references and index.
ISBN 978-1-56898-781-1 (pbk. : alk. paper)
1. Della Valle Bernheimer. 2. Architecture, Modern—20th century—
Themes, motives. 3. Architecture, Modern—21st century—Themes,
motives. I. Della Valle, Jared, 1971– II. Title.
NA737.D455A4 2009
720.92'2—dc22

                          2008055156

//

Contents

//

Acknowledgments

We owe a great deal to our teachers for the outlook of our firm, and we offer thanks to Adrian Luchini, Steven Leet, Xavier Vendrell, Bob Hansman, Ivan Zaknic, Christine Ussler-Trumbull, and Gerardo Caballero, who are each uniquely gifted instructors and architects. They provided direction to both of us as we embarked on our architectural educations, and they continue to inspire us. We are also indebted to our clients, who have allowed us the freedom to pursue the path of reinvention, and to our dedicated staff, who has helped us along this challenging course of investigation.

We are honored to be selected by Princeton Architectural Press and the Graham Foundation for inclusion in the New Voices in Architecture series. We would like to thank Kevin Lippert for giving us the chance to show our work, and we are particularly appreciative of Laurie Manfra's editorial dedication. We thank Stephen Cassell, Adam Yarinsky, Guy Nordenson, Brett Schneider, Aaron Betsky, and Mark Robbins for their thoughtful insights about our processes and work.

We are also grateful for the recognition that the Architectural League of New York, the Van Alen Institute, and the AIA New York Chapter have granted us over the past several years. We would like to thank Syracuse University, the Rhode Island School of Design, the City College of New York, and Lehigh University for allowing us to teach, as we continually draw inspiration from our devoted colleagues and energetic students of architecture.

Finally, it has been a privilege for us to work alongside many talented artists, architects, fabricators, and engineers throughout the first ten years of practice. We would like to acknowledge our many collaborators: Kari Anderson, Cathy Braasch, Brian Butterfield, Andrew Colopy, George Dawes, Dana Frankel, Jonathan Gonzalez, Ryan Harasimowicz, Erik Helgen, Gregory Horgan, Sarah Ingham, Garrick Jones, Tessie Nam, Matt Nowaczyk, Kate Patterson, A. J. Pires, Adam Ruedig, Javier Santamaria, Dylan Sauer, Burck Schellenberg, Lara Shihab Eldin, Suzanne Stefan, Andrew Willard, and Maxwell Worrell.

We especially want to offer our gratitude to Janine Soper for all of her tireless effort in helping create this book. We owe thanks to our professional colleagues: Architecture Research Office, Briggs Knowles Architecture + Design, Lewis.Tsurumaki.Lewis, Nat Oppenheimer (of Robert Silman Associates), Guy Nordenson Associates Structural Engineers, Mike Ra (of Front), and Steven Tupu (of Terrain). With special thanks to Frank Oudeman, Jock Pottle, Encore, and Peter Mauss for helping people "see" our work. We would also like to thank Richard Barnes, whose imagery has inspired us and whose photography has creatively captured the spaces we have made.

Andy: I would like to extend special thanks to my parents and sisters, who have all provided encouragement, motivation, support, intellect, and running commentary over the years. I would like to thank Mark Lamster for his constantly insightful critiques and good advice. I dedicate this book to Nicole, Isaac, and Alice, the best family one could ever hope for.

Jared: I would like to offer special thanks to my parents for giving me the motivation and support to achieve, and my brother Craig for setting the example. I would like to thank Katherine McConvey for trusting her instinct. I dedicate this book to my wife and best friend, Carolina, and my daughters Evia and Isa, for being so delicious.

—Andrew Bernheimer and Jared Della Valle

Preface

In the spring of 2008, Jared Della Valle and Andy Bernheimer taught the Judith Seinfeld Visiting Critic Studio, a series of classes focusing on housing and mixed-use developments, at Syracuse University's School of Architecture. Earlier that academic year, after discussing their work over dinner with the studio's sponsor, in New York City, it was perhaps a matter of luck that we were confronted with a billboard for 245 Tenth, the firm's darkly sleek residential project located along the heavily marketed edge of Chelsea, delimited on the west by the High Line. The glistening night-view rendering, posted near the site—at the time, the building was under construction, hidden behind fences—provided the ideal segue for our conversation about the work of Della Valle Bernheimer (DB) and their proposed studio, which was to be based on a seventy-story, mixed-use tower, sited further uptown, north of the Javits Center development. The students' work was to involve architectural investigations derived, at least in part, from the realities of the New York City real estate market.

Della Valle Bernheimer's projects are explorations of form and fabrication, investigations into the material properties of architecture. Beyond the intensity of attention to craft, they address the marketplace head-on and at close remove. For them, properties of architecture are always informed by the economic and material conditions of production. DB makes a convincing case for creating added value through design, acting as their own developers, a mode of practice that has seen a recent resurgence.

Their projects reflect a broad range of scale and intention, with the smallest being a seemingly fragile pavilion at the Philbrook Museum, in Tulsa, Oklahoma, where they cinematically morphed the shapes of butterfly wings through the computer to create a moiré shimmer of screens. Translating organic forms through digital technologies is a fascination of our age, but one of DB's earliest projects—a renovation of a Cape Cod–style house in Massachusetts—reinforces the sense that observation and the details of everyday life also provide motivating forces. This simple project sits on a modest plot, split in two by a change in cladding. It recalls the surface patterns found in older suburbs, where duplex houses are painted different colors or surfaced with brick on one, stucco on the other. A split of program on the inside is designated by an exterior change of skin. In this house, called Empty Nest, interior surfaces and volumes dissolve the usual configuration of rooms. Over time, the functions that define the house have changed to include a larger bedroom suite, study, and library, all occupying one volume, demarcated by a change of cladding on the outside. This visual gesture remakes the dwelling while utilizing the iconic geometries of the typical suburban house. The volume can be understood as sculptural, recalling the work of artist Joel Shapiro but having the intensity and humor of a Gordon Matta-Clark installation.

A few years later, DB worked on a challenging high-density site in East New York, Brooklyn. Acting as architects and developers for the Department of Housing Preservation and Development's New Foundations Program, which encourages private development of affordable housing, DB invited three firms—Architecture Research Office (ARO), Briggs Knowles Architecture + Design, and Lewis.Tsurumaki.Lewis—to collaborate on five two-family homes. Their objective was to address the difficulties of designing dense low-rise housing within a tight budget. They succeeded with a level of variation that is consistent with urban neighborhoods.

Dense low-rise housing has been a historical mainstay of Brooklyn and Queens, with acres of it sprawling outward from the city in the early part of the last century. Newer proposals for market-rate and subsidized housing, in general, never seem to get it right. Often, individual houses set back from the street are too horizontal and suburban, or they are too large and slablike to be anything but new enclaves with all the obvious earmarks of subsidized housing that is trying to "pass."

DB's housing project, as built, holds the street edge and respects the domestic scale, as opposed to pandering to some oddly misplaced mythology about home or family. Working with a vocabulary of resonant forms, the massing makes sense without duplicating the surrounding environment. Newness is addressed as a positive attribute within a preexisting community. This small-scale project is indicative of the goals of the firm; it reveals a keen awareness of the world, an awareness that does not abdicate the need for something projective or settle for a decorated pro forma solution.

Education happens through work like this. This is an important matter for our students and for those working in the private and civic realms to understand. Innovative approaches serve us better and make the case for the poetry and intelligence too rarely seen in our houses, schools, and public spaces. The trick is to find work that is financially sound, sustainable, and smart in terms of technology and construction and that also reads appropriately to different taste groups.

The project that launched Della Valle Bernheimer, 450 Golden Gate Plaza in San Francisco, reconfigured a public space and repositioned the federal presence in the city. A simple formal move—tilting a plane with an inscribed line that crosses the site diagonally—transformed the entrance of the building and achieved what they describe as a democratization of access. DB focuses on the intersections of public and private while addressing the real estate market, issues of financing, and matters of art; their teaching reflects this hybrid mix of practice. When Andy and Jared taught the Judith Seinfeld Visiting Critic Studio, they discussed the complexity, as well as the staggering costs, of their current projects. In response to a question about their capabilities of working on buildings of increasing scale, they responded in an optimistic tone, "Well, we didn't know exactly how to do those first projects when we did them. We just did them. There's a first time for everything." It was an indication that, for architects, experimentation and risk are part of our daily work. This was an ideal point of departure from which to talk about architecture, a place where everything seems possible.

—Mark Robbins, dean, Syracuse University School of Architecture

///

Pairs

Aaron Betsky

Della Valle Bernheimer likes to operate via combination. Having accepted the status of architecture as consisting of a series of tasks, including the organization of that particular and invisible phenomenon, space; the allocation of resources into a frame; and the production of skins within which space and material can appear, they revel in the manipulation of exactly those elements in such a manner that, as Jared Della Valle puts it, "a person who uses our buildings can recover what we put into it." To accomplish this, they have to leave their combinations evident. They also have to operate on the assembly itself, combining development and design while working in collaboration with allied firms. They eschew the expression of large social, technical, or aesthetic issues. They focus only on the work itself and proceed by articulation, composition, and contrast. The result is an architecture of effects that are clear though not always obvious. Simple lines and boxes shift, slide, or dematerialize in order, above all else, to make one aware of their presence. They are in balance but never resolved.

The professional twosome of Della Valle and Bernheimer seems to like working in pairs. Take, for instance, the two houses they designed for themselves and their families, Bernheimer's in upstate New York and Della Valle's in Fire Island. The latter is simpler, an existing house cleaned up, opened, and clad in wood and zinc. Metal dominates the house, abstracting the volume while emphasizing a larger cubical mass and small structure extending over the deck, where the wood siding and deck merge and the base appears to reach up and grab hold of the house. The gestures are simple and economical, reflecting the tastes of an architect who has degrees in both construction management and architecture and who codevelops buildings in Manhattan.

The Bernheimer house, by contrast, is a more complex affair. Also clad in a combination of wood and metal, in this instance copper, it consists of a longer space with three saw-toothed skylights and a cubic volume similar to that of the Della Valle house. Bernheimer delights in the ability of copper to weather and discolor, while Della Valle desires a more consistent appearance. The complex shapes of Bernheimer's home find their counterpart in

Copper House, Columbia County, N.Y.   Zinc House, Fire Island, N.Y.

///

windows positioned to catch particular fragments of the landscape, incorporating views into the interior as found art. Its complexities may derive from the fact that it is a stand-alone piece of new construction, not a renovation, but the two houses do represent different elements of the partners' work.

The spatial gymnastics inherent in the Bernheimer house, for instance, spin out in the Artreehoose in New Fairfield, Connecticut, completed in 2008. Wood-clad volumes extend into space, held together by a steel frame that becomes evident as the scaffolding for the living spaces in the house's interior. Della Valle and Bernheimer clad the house with board and batten, which acts as an abstraction of traditional building materials. Interior volumes extend the logic of both the balloon frame of the standard suburban home and the cubic composition of high modernism. The house is exuberant in its spatial and volumetric effects and yet tightly controlled, disciplined, rooted in memory, and reserved in appearance.

By contrast, the housing they designed in 2005 in East New York, Brooklyn, as part of a City of New York program to provide affordable dwelling units, reduces most of the effects to plays with the facade. Inside, the houses are as generous as financing and building codes would allow, which is to say, not very. Outside, Della Valle and Bernheimer created a sense of scale and identity simply by contrasting metal siding with horizontal and vertical corrugations, as well as by grouping standard windows and cladding small areas in wood. On one facade, they were able to manipulate the volume sufficiently to produce a cross-shaped profile protruding from the box.

A third residential structure, a renovation completed in 2005 in Fire Island, New York, sums up DB's strategy. It is a wooden box contained by a bold lintel that wraps around to become an exterior wall and sill—a modernist line, implying a box, that contains a volume. Its practical, familiar form is indicated by the use of wood siding. Again by contrast, the renovation of architect Paul Rudolph's own house on Beekman Place in New York City, completed in 2006, is nothing but lines and voids, the actual forms having been reduced to white planes

23 Beekman Place, N.Y.   Fire Island Residence, Fire
Island, N.Y.

///

Artreehoose, New Fairfield, Conn.   Glenmore Gardens, East New
York, N.Y.

///

hovering in air. Della Valle and Bernheimer brought out the freedom from gravity and containment that Rudolph worked so hard to achieve in all of his buildings, as a reflection of an almost utopian modernist thirst for liberation that he was only able to bring to some resolution through relentless tinkering on his own house.

To extend these comparisons to a larger scale, consider DB's two condominium towers located a few blocks from each other in New York City's Chelsea neighborhood. While the 459 West 18th Street building is a clear illustration of zoning and financial conditions, which divide the form into two contrasting pieces, one clad in white and the other in black glass; the 245 Tenth Avenue tower absorbs these complexities into a deformed shape, while its facade is composed of a pixelated grid of glass and metal panels. It bows out slightly, asserting its presence over the High Line, a disused rail yard currently being transformed into a park, just as its skin dematerializes. Like 459 West 18th Street, the tower is L-Shaped, its two volumes only barely seeming to touch. One is never quite sure whether the Tenth Avenue building is really there, but at the same time, it cannot be avoided. The Eighteenth Street building, by contrast, has a simpler shape that shifts into two slices. The tall white volume recedes into the background as an abstract block; ribbon windows give it some sense of scale. The lower block, by contrast, is darker than its surroundings; the same lines of windows slice open what appears to be an otherwise closed volume. It is as if Della Valle and Bernheimer took the properties inherent in the surrounding buildings; emphasized them; made them simpler and clearer, including the sloped eaves and setbacks; and balanced them out so that one can clearly understand their innate tendencies.

DB's most ambitious project to date, the eighty-two-story Hudson Yards Tower, might seem a far remove from the modest garden pavilion they designed for the Philbrook Museum in Tulsa, Oklahoma, in 2004, but both designs emphasize the dematerialization of skin while asserting the presence of either the real or implied block. The tower is split into two slabs, with the higher one rising up toward the rear; a glass-enclosed stack of bridges connects

459 West 18th, New York, N.Y.   245 Tenth, New York, N.Y.   Migration Tower, New York, N.Y.   Butterfly Pavilion, Tulsa, Okla.

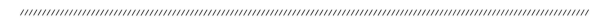

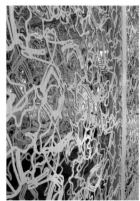

the two. Della Valle and Bernheimer extended the separation of geometric volumes—corresponding to the zoning envelope—to both a larger scale and a higher degree of abstraction. The facade is meant to disappear into a cloudlike apparition, reminiscent of a flock of birds, as if the architects were sculpting nothing but ephemeral matter, not a massive skyscraper. By contrast, the pavilion at the Philbrook Museum tries to make the ephemeral present. Its laser-cut metal skin, based on the shape of a butterfly, dissolves into a filigreed container of space, implied by the manner in which these white panels assemble themselves around a rectangular wood podium, wrapping to create a ceiling that evokes the pattern of leaves from surrounding trees. In both of these projects, Della Valle and Bernheimer beg the question of what the solid core of architecture should be. Is it a building that can be occupied, or is it the assembly of material toward an effect that recalibrates the occupant's relation to his or her surroundings, whether natural or human made?

In DB's design for the tables on which their firm works in their Brooklyn loft, completed in 2005, the architecture becomes a landscape carved into the tops, while the scissoring legs and articulated supports allow for a modular assembly. The whorls of the tabletop are intended to reflect and house the ephemeral objects particular to each designer, from drafting tools to cellular phones and iPods. These landscapes are structures that articulate and accommodate work, just as the design of an office building might, but they do their task at a much smaller scale and with a medium that we might not think of as proper to the field of architecture. Yet their forms are clearly related to Della Valle and Bernheimer's 2001 competition entry to design an aquatic center in Aalborg, Denmark. Here, the whirling table becomes a plane of water, cut into what is otherwise just a rectangular box. It makes the fluid nature of water present, accommodates the splashing and swimming occupants, and, in general, gives form to that which is formless.

These two projects show Della Valle and Bernheimer developing a horizontal version of the dissolving form through the use of remarkably solid materials, which has become a

JACK Table   Aquacenter, Aalborg, Denmark

///

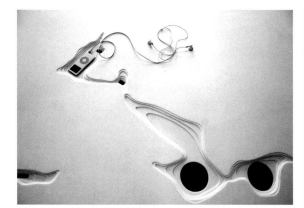
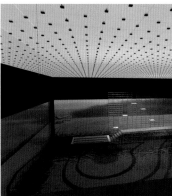

hallmark of their architecture. In a sense, this is where they started and where they may continue. In 1996, they won the competition for the redesign of San Francisco's Federal Plaza; its folded forms re-emerge and find their pairing in the rising grass roof of the 2007 Maine State Pier competition entry. In the plaza, the architecture consisted of what was, essentially, the roof of an underground parking garage that the architects manipulated to provide a series of amenities, such as benches, as well as to differentiate and create shelter within an otherwise windswept public space. The jagged landscape sliced and diced the plane—we don't usually see it because we occupy it as we move—and created a series of relationships between the surrounding buildings. In Maine, DB created a building that simply disappears beneath the green park rising from the foot of the pier, extending over the building's various functions and arriving at a point that can be a belvedere or lookout point comparable in scale and height to the cruise liners that dock there. The building's actual volume is just a glass box, but the architecture is no more or less than the plane from which architecture usually starts (or is absent from) articulated into form.

Pair by pair, though not in temporal progression, Della Valle and Bernheimer seem to be moving toward an architecture that is both present and absent, both skin and volume. What is missing is the articulation of structure, the monumentality of built form, a hierarchy of building elements, and a sense of expressive experimentation with technology or typology. You might say that Della Valle and Bernheimer work with the materials and programs at hand and try to tease out some sense of the institution or client's character, while using an array of tried-and-true materials and responding with care to the surroundings. That does not mean that their buildings either disappear into tradition or their surroundings. Rather, they are exemplars of what we might now think of as the classical modern canon. In fulfilling the aims and methods of that particular mode, Della Valle and Bernheimer find satisfaction in doing what they can with a great deal of skill. They play it pretty straight and, as a result, the work is perfectly balanced. Yet somehow, out of a clear-headed confrontation with the act of building and development comes recognizable and beautiful architecture.

Maine State Pier, Portland, Maine

450 Golden Gate Plaza, San Francisco, Calif.

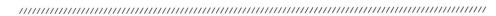

Think/Make

Midway through Steven Spielberg's sci-fi masterpiece *Close Encounters of the Third Kind*, Roy Neary, played by Richard Dreyfuss, tears into a pile of potatoes, sculpting them into a facsimile of the natural wonder Devils Tower. His replica volcanic outcropping "means something," but he admits, he does not know what. Instinct leads him to making, and making raises the question of meaning. But his intuition remains indescribable. The very personal significance of his tower of tubers eludes explanation.

This is the dilemma of our architecture. How do you make something meaningful out of an instinct of thinking and then have that meaning be recognizable to others? This takes a certain trust in potatoes. For some, a potato will always be just a potato. But for us, it's something to devour, to sculpt, and to know. It's a poignant vegetable; a misshapen figure that, in its earthy weight and lumpy being, makes us feel some kind of strange wonder. Like an idea, it grows in hidden fashion and must be unearthed.

Our firm evolved instinctively. In 1995, we were working for others in the architecture and construction fields when we stumbled, quite literally, on an announcement in a bookshop for a design competition for the renovation of a federal plaza in San Francisco. For thirty-five dollars we could test our relationship as designers (and friends) and possibly get a built project out of it; this was our immediate thinking. For us, the key premise of the competition was that the winning proposal might be built. We were young and naive. We didn't consider this a stock disclaimer of most architectural competitions. We immediately thought of the project as real.

When we returned the entry fee, we had already calculated our odds of success: Perhaps there would be 200 applicants, and maybe we were smarter than half of them. That made our odds one in a hundred, not bad considering that we had learned in our professional practice courses that only one in fourteen interviews for potential work by accomplished professional firms ends in success.

"This means something. This is important."
From *Close Encounters of the Third Kind*

To our surprise (and against the real odds, which are painstakingly known now that we are out in the world), we won. That lucky moment fomented our trust in intuition. We were interviewed by the General Services Administration, along with several other winners, and eventually selected to execute the design. At the time, we were unlicensed, working out of a toxic metal shop with an atrophied dog named Snoop always lying on the cement floor, and designing a 45,000-square-foot public space with nearly full artistic freedom. We were actually making something.

The design for 450 Golden Gate Plaza, the second project of our collaboration, relied on a single mechanism: a folded plane that bent and moved in accordance with the site's access requirements, the Americans with Disabilities Act building code, and the security needs of the United States Marshals Service, as well as the natural elements of wind and light. This folded plane also accommodated a surface treatment for a publicly curated collage, representing a participatory act of local architecture, the patterns and textural qualities of which remain prevalent in our work twelve years later. To this day, we have remained committed to investigating the indeterminate relationship between site, function, and client. We start with a word, maybe a concept, probably a noun. Language evolves into making, and intuition and mechanical doing are entwined by thinking.

Think empty nest; make an addition: A renovation and expansion of a home in suburban Boston for an empty-nest couple addressed the ingrained habits of over thirty years of living, and it literally extrudes these habits in formal terms. The new construction stretches the shape of the existing colonial house and wraps it in zinc, instead of cedar.

Think building on tracks; make steam clouds for train: A billowy building adjacent to the proposed High Line park in Manhattan evokes the image of steam clouds from foregone railroad cars. The skin of the building is composed of a literal image of clouds fabricated out of punched stainless steel.

Think trees; make tree house: A modern lakeside house in Connecticut reveals its structure of steel and long-span plywood, evoking the language of exposed timber construction and tying itself, metaphorically, to the trees that surround it.

Think table; make leg: A modular structure, made out of cast aluminum and crafted through a process of extensive research, engages computer numerical control (CNC) technology to make a single, economical table leg that is adaptable to countless desk configurations.

Think clock; make timepiece: A house wrapped in copper, in upstate New York, measures the passage of time. It ages visibly on the exterior as the material transforms over the years, while skylights on the interior track the hours of the day.

Think pavilion; make cocoon: A garden folly in Tulsa, Oklahoma, explores the etymology of the word *pavilion* in order to derive a pattern of butterflies and create a cocoon for its occupants.

In the formative moments of each project, a reduction of expression exists, for us, as a counterbalance to the prototypical and expansive aspects of architecture. Most of our buildings are effectively the first and last of their kind. Usually, they are made by proven methodologies that have been tested by us; however, unless deployed in a repeated fashion, each project is a one-off, never to be rebuilt. (Just as a thought only truly exists in the moment that it happens, and no other.) We aim to mitigate risk via several thought-gestures: by a reduction of systems, through stringent research into new methods of fabrication beyond the common, and through the simplification of architectural language. After the initial moment of instinct, we think through ways of making, while intellectual and mechanical mental associations play crucial roles.

We also search for a "distillation of thought," which we believe makes spaces and designs accessible and enriching, even if our authorial intentions are not, on the surface, legible to others. Everyone's intuition is different, but if the design is well articulated, we can enter each other's thought-spaces. Our architecture is a kind of syllogism, where primary elements and secondary textures combine, legibly and intuitively, to guide users to their own distinctive and diverse responses. While motifs and themes, such as specific technical strategies, may reappear over time throughout our work, each project's parti is inherently related to the specifics and differences of site and client, and they will be re-created by the users over time.

We strive to always think anew—to make each project unlike any that preceded it. The absence of an overarching signature is not an earth-shattering pronouncement on our part; rather, it liberates us. We believe in consistency, not homogeneity. We have thought through the business side of our impulses, and this has allowed us, as practitioners, to proactively expand the rules of development within our firm in the spirit of instinctual thinking and making. We have cultivated relationships with developers and independent sources of financing, which have given us an elevated degree of control over the inception of projects and an increased likelihood of their being realized. We have acted as developers, inventing opportunities for affordable housing and market-rate construction and seeing these efforts through, in most cases, to the point of breaking ground. We have engaged the field of product design, partnering with manufacturing companies to create custom products for our own office as well as for several real estate development properties. We love to live in the things we make; it is where we live, inside our minds, and we are deeply appreciative for opportunities to make things for others.

This spirit was rooted in us over a decade ago. In graduate school, we had the good fortune of learning from immensely talented professors, who were not only teachers, but active builders. Their work ranged from small apartments to public spaces and large-scale urban projects. They all drew beautifully and conceptualized rigorously. They privileged the act of making, but not at the expense of thinking. The first question they posed to us was, "What were you thinking?" The second was, "How would you build it?" We were thus ingrained, from the first moments of our architectural educations, with a sense of intellectual responsibility to the made object, by the people who made it. This taught us to be mindful of being mindful.

Our diverse practice is rooted in an ongoing effort to invent and formulate projects and to create a world where others may also live. We seek to make things that are thoughtful, interpretive, and substantial, even as we search, like Roy Neary, to explain what we mean.

—Andrew Bernheimer and Jared Della Valle

//

245 Tenth

A 54,000-square-foot residential tower in the Chelsea arts district of Manhattan contains nineteen apartments and two galleries. The design uses images of the old steam trains that traversed the High Line tracks, adjacent to the site, to derive form and surface. Our initial studies were of clouds emanating from the smokestacks of railroad cars. Dissipating into the sky, these clouds tended to have dark, thick tones at their bases and then would billow, dissolve, and lighten into the sky. Their vaporous, tonal metamorphoses inform both the architectural form of the building and the texture of its skin, through embossing.

To replicate the phenomena of clouds, we made several digital studies of a steam engine cloud and isolated a small area depicting the gradient from black to white. This area was then pixelated and overlaid onto the facade in accordance with a variety of contextual conditions pertaining to privacy, view, and light. Five types of pixels were designed and then transformed from dots to protruding diamonds, for capturing light. Custom dies for a CNC turret punch (like a large-scale typewriter) were manufactured. As two-by-four-foot panels run through the machine, a digital drawing instructs it to punch each piece of stainless steel with a pattern of diamonds, reimaging and transposing the cloud across the facade of the building. These raised diamonds catch light differently throughout the day and year; though fixed materially, each facade is a mutable surface. The building's color, shade, and depth are untethered. In this way, ornament is inextricable from architecture; while environment and site history are emblazoned in a dichotomy in which local context is fixed, even while construction is ever-changing.

Steam train precedent   Pixelated steam cloud

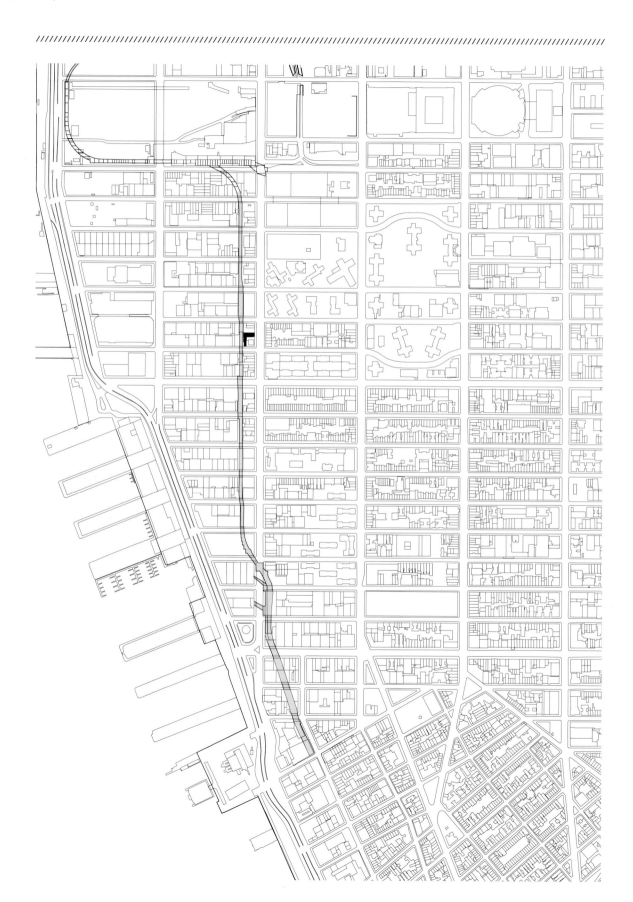

//

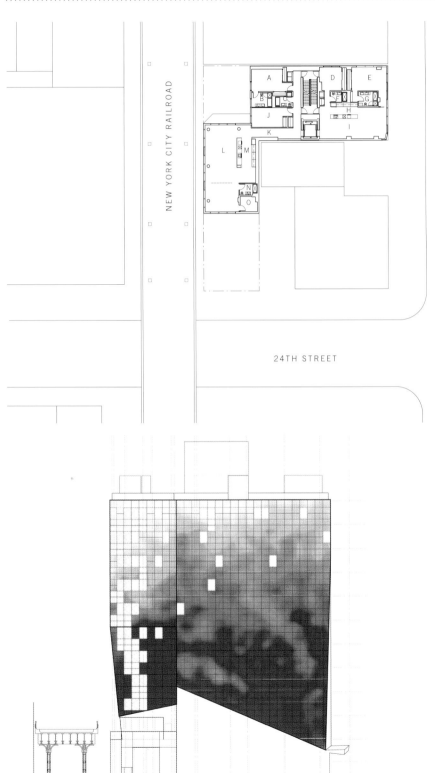

A　Master Bedroom
B　Master Bathroom
C　Bathroom
D　Office
E　Master Bedroom
F　Bathroom
G　Master Bathroom
H　Kitchen
I　Living/Dining
J　Bedroom
K　Gallery
L　Living/Dining
M　Kitchen
N　Bath
O　Mechanical Storage

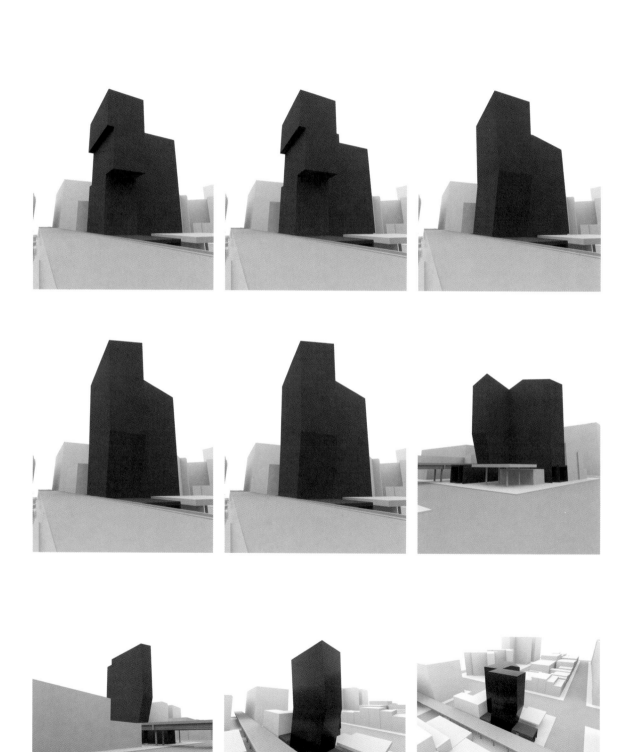

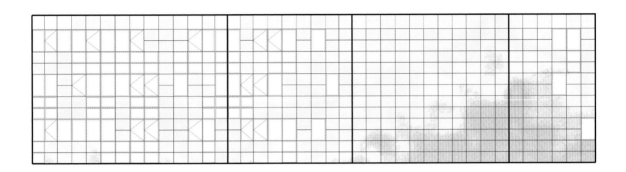

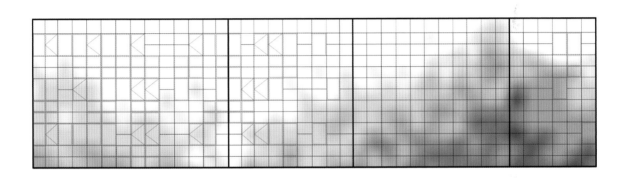

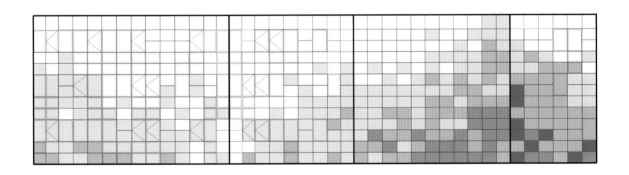

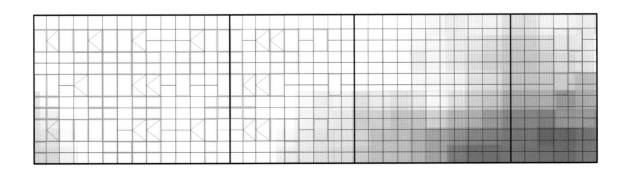

A   Rainscreen gasket
B   Silicone sealant and backer rod
C   Thermal insulator
D   Rain screen gasket
E   Stack joint splice book (silicone sheet)
F   Isolator gasket
G   Mullion plug (PVC foam 15 lbs. per cubic ft.)
H   Interior glazing gasket
I   Hex-head bolt with flat washer and nylon hex-lock nut
J   Custom-embossed stainless steel panel with diamond pattern
K   Stick pin
L   Aluminum panel
M   Load-lifting alignment lug
N   1 ½" foil tape around perimeter
O   Interior aluminum closure

P   White silicone at perimeter
Q   Stack joint gutter boot (PVC/flush-glazed system)
R   Stack-joint air and water seal gasket
S   Hex-nylon lock nut
T   Silicone sealant
U   Leveler bolt
V   Fire safety with poured-smoke stop
W   Hex-head cap screw with flat washer and nylon hex-lock nut
X   M12 nylon nut
Y   Concrete insert
Z   1 × 1 angle
a   Silicone sealant
b   Concrete embed pocket
c   Face of concrete

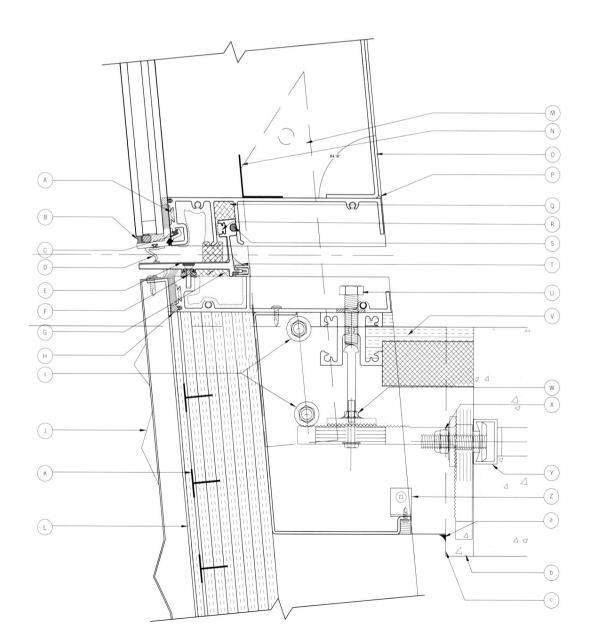

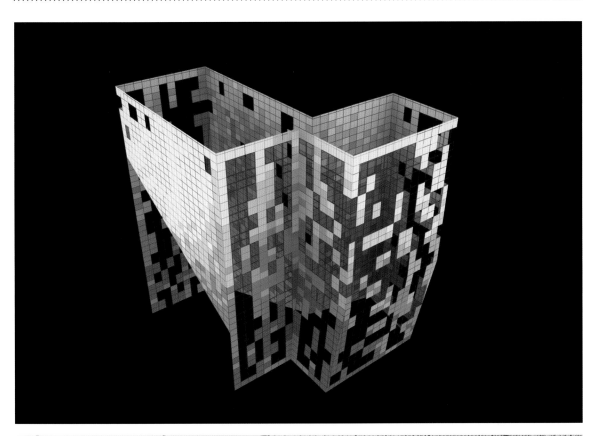

//

//

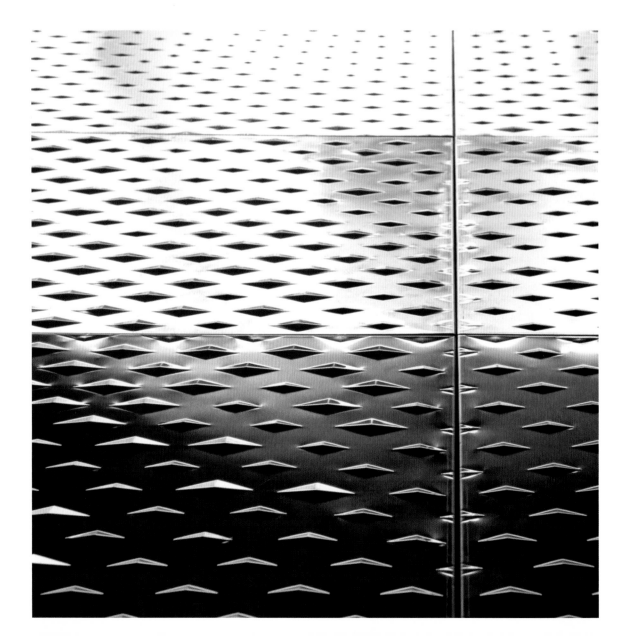

459 West 18th

The primary architectural expression for this building involves two interlocking volumes. Nesting black-and-white shapes reveal the zoning requirements of the Special West Chelsea District. These shapes are not sculpted to defy requirements; rather, they embrace and then hyperarticulate these constraints. On an experiential level, the design intention was to construct a solid building that would give occupants a panoramic connection to the city. We also sought to avoid fabricating a normative piece of modern architecture, the glass box. Simultaneously, we examined the modern precedent of "colorless" architecture made from metal and glass, materials that, in primary form, impart no color or tonal gradients on the artifice they define. Our first studies were of binary conditions or architecture made from opposites. Several iterations of orthogonal blocks were composed, with the final form assuming the shape of the idealized zoning diagram.

While many new buildings express visual connectivity to the city through ubiquitous expanses of transparent surfaces—for example, a new building on an adjacent property is composed of folded planes of floor-to-ceiling curtain-wall glass—our design posits that a solid, totemic object can be equally revealing. The facade presents swatches of voids. Extruded aluminum collars hold enormous expanses of unbroken, seamless glass. In this way, the window becomes a minimal yet severe vitrine that is mostly invisible but forces spatial containment. The monumental openings, measuring as large as eight-by-eighteen feet, take the background of the city and place it at the forefront of one's experience. The windows, engineered by facade consultants Front Inc. and fabricated by Via Glass, are detailed with this minimalist aesthetic in mind. Mullions are only two inches thick, and the frame for the vent is nested within the mullion to conceal its operating mechanisms. All hardware disappears, while interruptions within glass expanses are kept to a minimum. The building is thus articulated as a pair of linked or nested dualities: solid and void, black and white.

Black-and-white cookie

Sketch

///

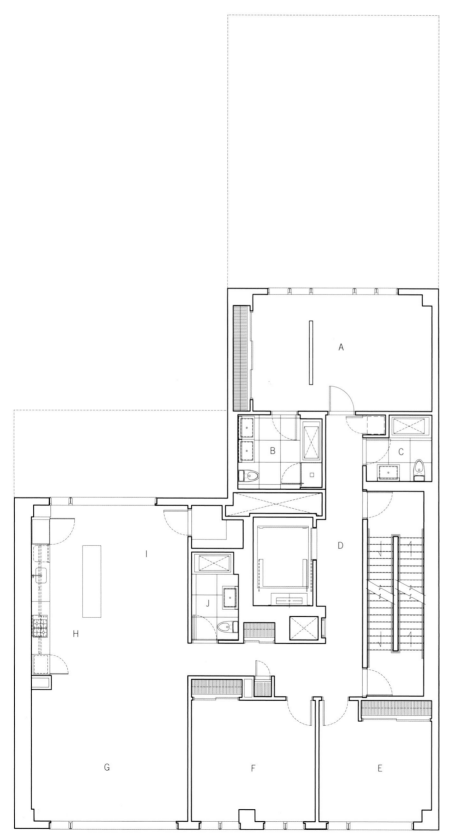

A   Master Bedroom
B   Bathroom
C   Bathroom
D   Foyer
E   Bedroom
F   Bedroom
G   Living Room
H   Kitchen
I   Dining Room
J   Bathroom

//

///

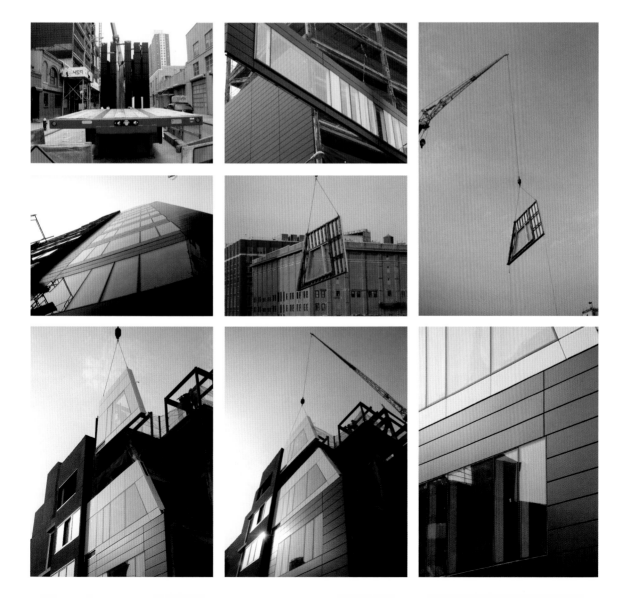

Butterfly Pavilion

Our design for a garden structure for the Philbrook Museum of Art finds its origins in the spirit and etymology of the word *pavilion*, which derives from the Latin *papilion*, meaning butterfly. Our cocoonlike structure is also inspired by the entomological transformation of the silkworm, a *Bombyx mori* caterpillar, into the silkmoth. In an act of becoming, the larva pupates, spinning itself an intricate chamber. Inside nature's self-made garden structure, it transforms into a winged moth, eventually leaving its tiny cocoon of spun silk.

Our pavilion creates an artificial cocoon, not spun of silk but etched and cut from plate steel. Using laser-cutting technology, we constructed a diminutive eight-by-sixteen-foot pavilion fabricated structurally from wood decking and steel tubes. Two layers of quarter-inch-thick panels, powder coated on the outer layer in white and on the inner layer in sky blue, are attached to the structure. Etched into these panels is the repeated and abstracted pattern of a butterfly wing, which filters light to create an artificial cocoonlike space, perfect for single occupancy. Light passing through these patterned walls creates a latticework of dappled illumination and shadow, providing the visitor with a space that maintains a gentle visual connection to the museum grounds. At night, the pavilion transforms into a lantern that casts a soft, diffuse glow.

Silkmoth cocoon   Initial butterfly   Solid versus void   Tracing

//

opposite

top: Laser-cut styrene mock-up

bottom left: Base structure

bottom center: With decking

bottom right: With cladding

//

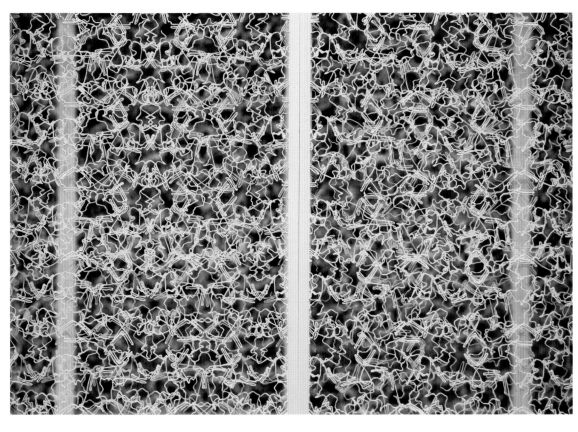

 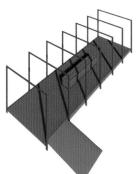 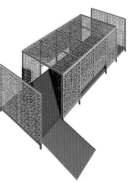

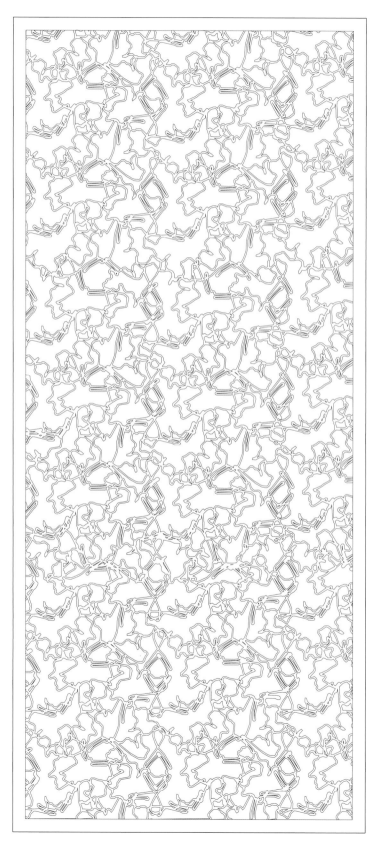

//

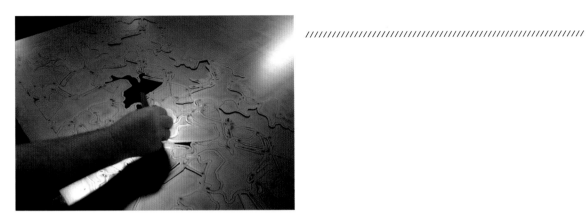

//

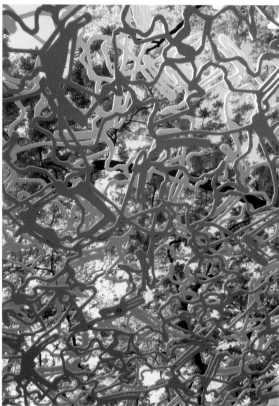

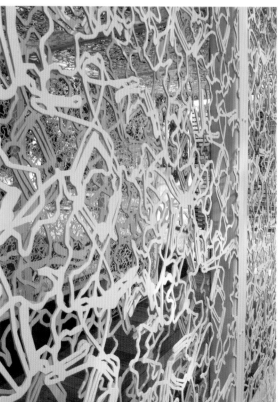

Artreehoose

Wedged into a tight lot on Lake Candlewood in New Fairfield, Connecticut, Artreehoose's form and structure were derived from observations of trees and local building techniques and from a stipulation that the house occupy the identical footprint of a previously existing structure. The project began with studies of leaf canopies, accumulated ring structures, and dappled light filtering through clusters of trees. Multiple study models in concrete, acrylic, wood, and plaster were employed to investigate the flow of light through perforated materials. We used these models to make secondary observations and to explore how certain materials could create a stable but discretely minimal structure. During the formative process, we were interested in designing a house that seemed, in large part, to float while also offering protection to its inhabitants, much the same way the surrounding tree canopies provide shelter.

The final design, a house measuring 5,400 square feet, was the result of intense collaboration with Guy Nordenson and Associates Structural Engineers, with whom we developed a unique structural system of long-span plywood joists functioning in tandem with a series of steel Vierendeel trusses and billets. Made from scarf-jointed Douglas fir, the joists were assembled into four-foot-wide panels, relying on steel stiffening pipes to join and stabilize the plywood prior to lifting them in place. The steel truss structure and joist system rest on slim columns, which support the cantilevered, red-cedar-clad volumes. The cedar was deployed using two different techniques: First, the vertical board-and-batten technique exaggerates the stacked appearance of the house, similar to the rings of a tree; and second, tongue-and-groove boards on the obverse facades expose the smooth surface of these metaphorical rings.

Organized around a central double-height volume and spanned by long-span joists, the ground floor is wrapped in monumental sliding glass panels, which open the house and connect the inside, quite literally, to the outside. The mobility of these panels exaggerates the weight of the cantilevered volumes. Like a tree trunk, a stairwell wrapped in American Black Walnut anchors the second-floor media room and is adjacent to a terrace (a void in the composition) that serves as an outdoor theater in summer. Also upstairs, two cantilevers contain the bedrooms, which protrude into the surrounding trees and extend over the lake like the prow of a boat. Carefully positioned skylights illuminate the great room and upstairs spaces.

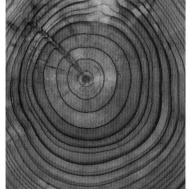

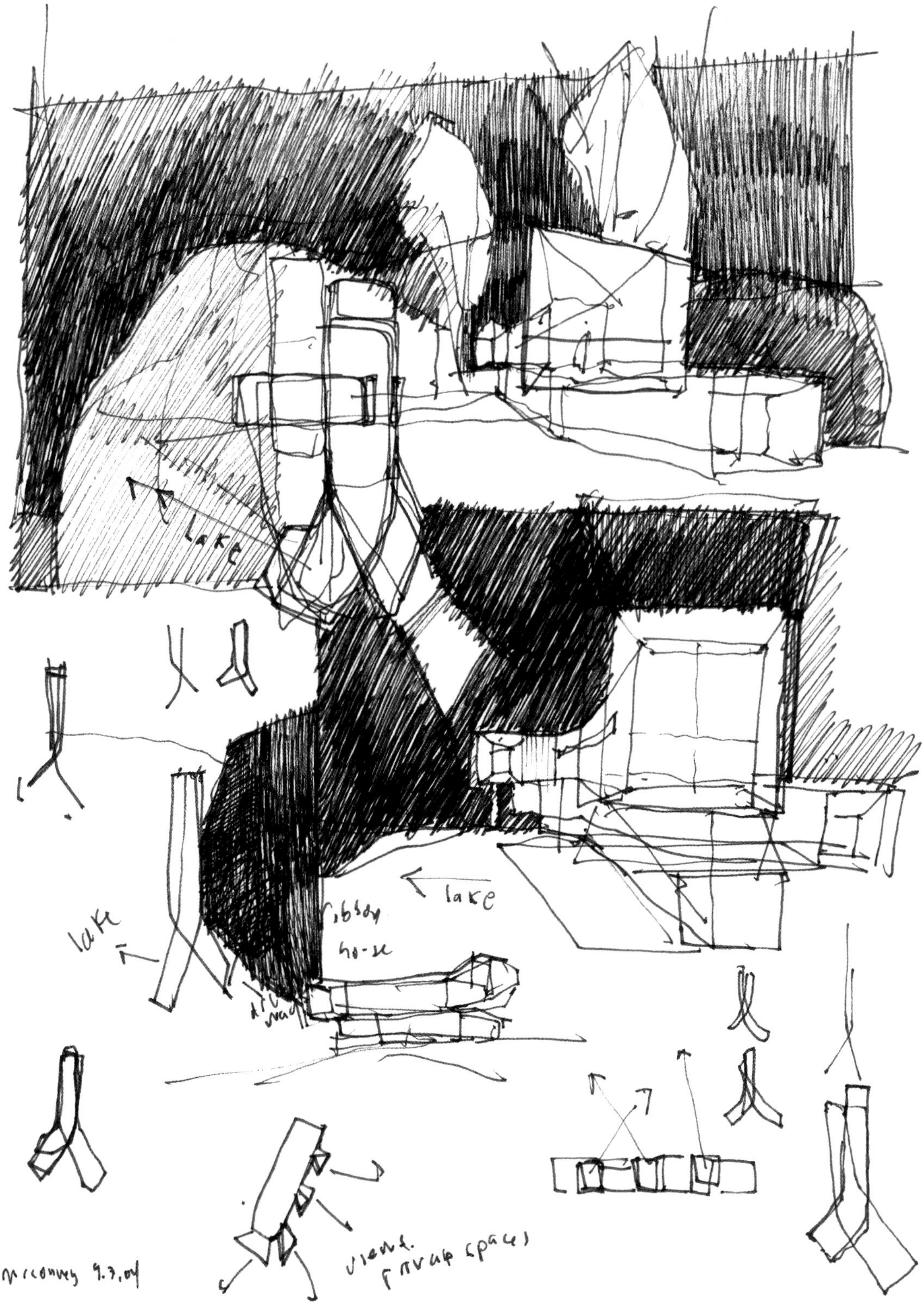
lake
lake
lake

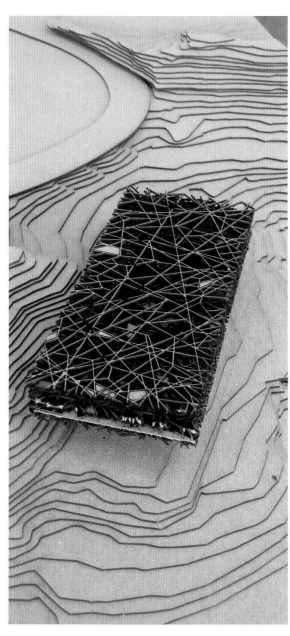

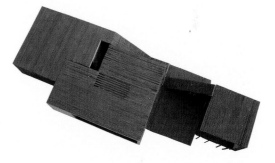

A Tale of Two Challenges

Guy Nordenson and Brett Schneider

The structural design of the Artreehoose is a tale of two challenges: one being a direct solution and the second requiring greater invention. The first challenge was to find a way to support the "opaque" bedrooms that cantilever over the "transparent" living spaces. The structure was accomplished using steel trusses supported by minimum-depth columns. The second challenge involved integrating the structure into a roof system designed to filter natural light, similar to the canopy of trees surrounding the site. The roof structure consists of closely spaced vertical joists made of exposed plywood, with skylights in certain locations.

The upper-floor cantilever required an adequately stiff structure for support and minimal columns at the ground floor to maintain transparency. Diagonalized steel trusses, with Vierendeel panels where necessary for doors, were hidden in the walls of the two suspended volumes. At the intersection of these spaces (where the bath and other service rooms are located), ground-level bracing provides lateral support.

For the minimal-support trusses, we considered several options. Our initial proposal was to anchor the structure to a rock adjacent to the house; however, this strategy proved too complex and only provided a reaction to the south cantilever. The final solution involved the use of exposed solid-steel-bar columns—two inches deep and four to six inches wide—inset from the glass along the south and west perimeters of the ground floor. Similar in size to the mullions of the glazing system, the columns typically align with their long, east-west dimension. At the interior corner formed by the two cantilevers, the column was offset to further disguise its supportive role.

The more complicated problem was the design of an integrated structure to accommodate the double-height "canopy" of the central space. During one of our initial meetings, discussion turned to Norwegian architect Sverre Fehn's Nordic Pavilion for the 1962 Venice Biennale, which featured concrete joists that remained open to the sky. We applied a similar structure of closely spaced plywood joists, measuring one inch wide and sixteen inches deep, to span the twenty-six-foot width of the main space and adjacent master bedroom. The final joists are composed of twelve-foot planks, spliced using staggered, full-depth scarf joints. Steel pipes threaded though the joists provide additional lateral stability and allow prefabrication in four-foot-wide panels, for greater control. The close spacing of the joists (six inches on center) limited the connection to the steel framing at the east and west ends to every other joist, using pipes to provide shear transfer to the connected joists.

Design was only half of the process. Further challenges occurred during construction, in particular, supporting the joists in a web of perimeter steel framing meant that the last section to be placed would not swing into place easily. The contractor chose not to prefabricate the panels, opting to install them individually using shoring and a temporary floor. The final panel was assembled and raised on site, with the end-connection plates being cut and mechanically spliced to allow us to swing it into place.

left top: Structural study of the steel superstructure and prototypical wood joist system

left center and bottom: Force-reaction diagrams

right top: Study model

right center: Steel superstructure

right bottom: Wood joist system

//

//

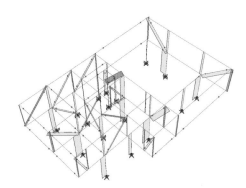

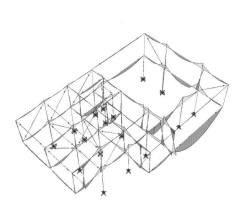

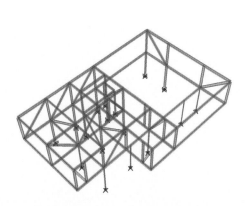

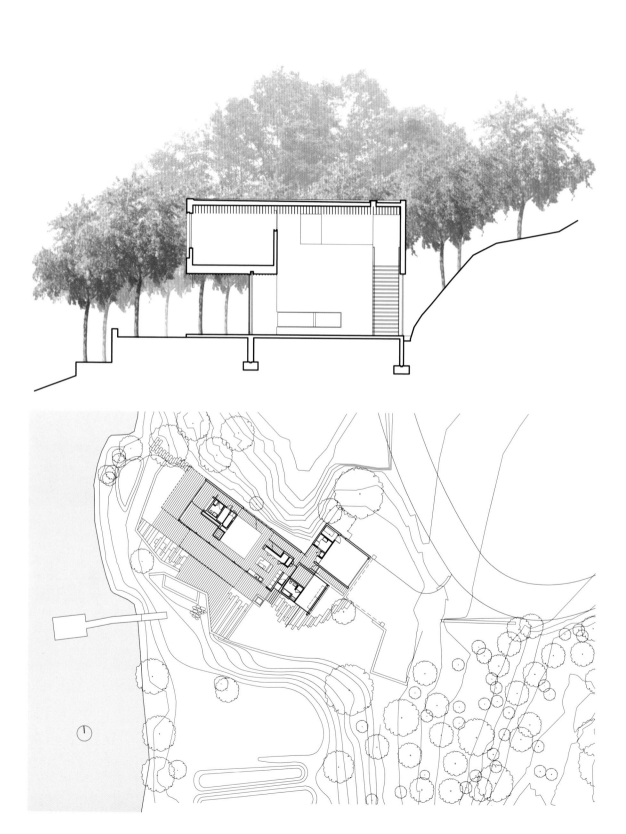

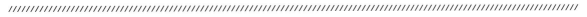

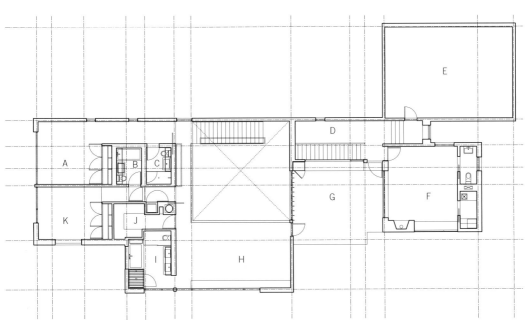

A	Bedroom	F	Home Theater
B	Bathroom	G	Roof Terrace
C	Bathroom	H	Master Bedroom
D	Balcony	I	Master Bathroom
E	Attic	J	Bedroom

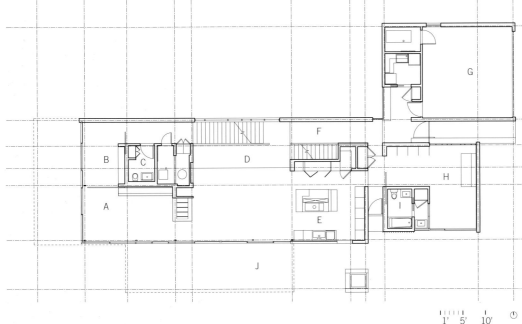

A	Dining Room	F	Entry
B	Office	G	Garage
C	Bathroom	H	Play Room
D	Great Room	I	Bathroom
E	Kitchen	J	Patio

top: Entry to kitchen and outdoor theater

bottom left: View from dining room toward kitchen

bottom right: Western cantilever

overleaf: Cantilevered master bedroom, view from terrace

//

Copper House

A weekend residence for a family of four, this house was conceived as a time-tracking device for registering day-to-day environmental changes and measuring the transformations of a nuclear family over months, years, and decades.

The house is sited on a wooded six-acre plot in the Hudson Valley, two hours north of New York City. The residence combines conventional compartmentalized living with a modern sense of loose boundaries. The ground floor is arranged around a twenty-four-foot-long bookshelf, a library composed of a single, ever-changing wall of shifting porosity. As the family collects more books, the wall will become more solid, and as the family rearranges them, it changes character. The library also separates the main entry and stair from the house's central social spaces (the kitchen, dining room, and living room).

These spaces, occupying the center of the house on the south facade, are lit indirectly from above by fixed monitors oriented to specific cardinal points. Because the dining room receives most of its light at dusk, its monitor faces west. Alternatively, the kitchen skylight is oriented to capture early morning light. A monitor in the guest room on the west side of the house faces east; it, too, receives morning sunlight. Protruding out of the north side of the house, a home office allows the parents to work while their children play outside.

The form of the building is composed both physically and metaphorically as a simple block, altered by the sun. The north volume remains whole, while notches on the south side are carved to correspond to the placement of skylights. Windows throughout the house are located according to views of specific trees and the surrounding forest. Clad primarily in vertically oriented corrugated-copper siding and a mixture of flat- and standing-seam copper roofing, the color and texture of the house evolves in response to climate. This aging process is meant to echo the metamorphosis and growth of the family that inhabits the house.

Patinas of copper cladding

///

   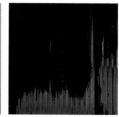 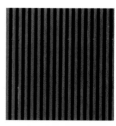

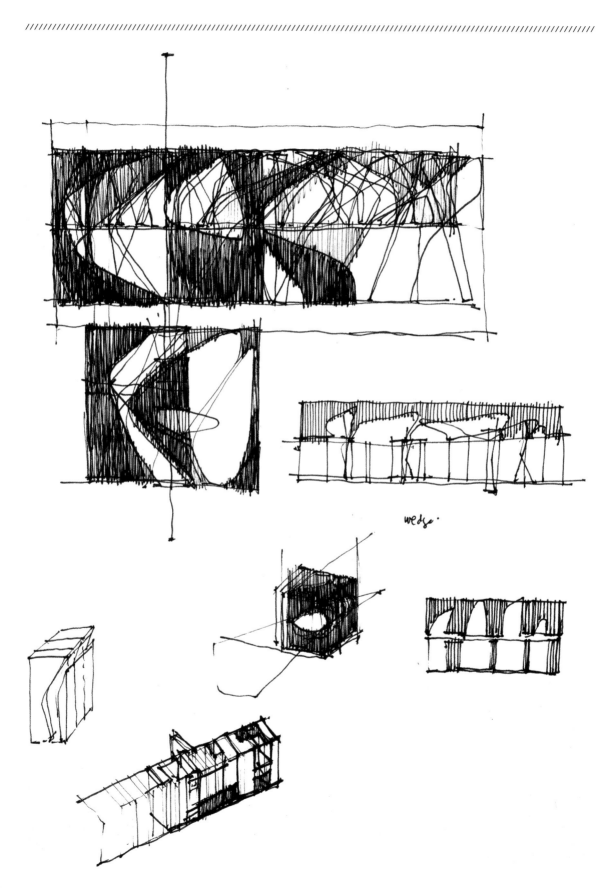

wedge.

///

A   Storage
B   Playroom
C   Library
D   Bathroom
E   Bedroom

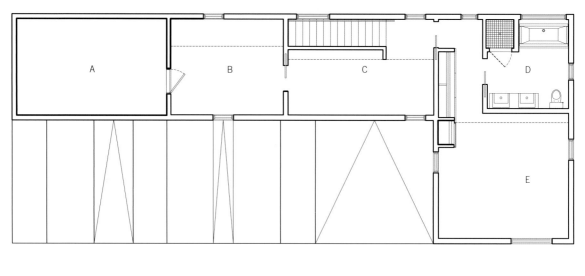

A   Bedroom   D   Office   G   Living Room
B   Bathroom   E   Bathroom   H   Dining Room
C   Library   F   Bedroom   I   Kitchen

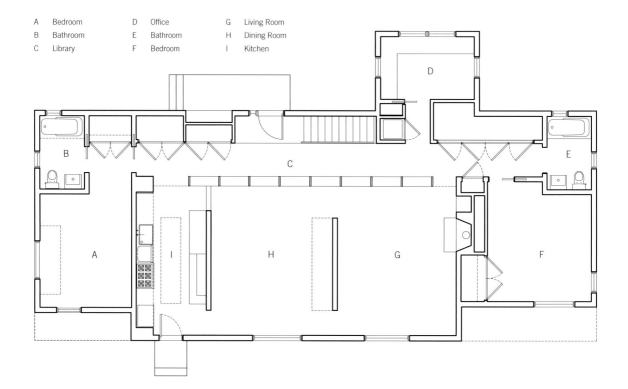

//

//

A   Copper coping
B   Switched exhaust fan to vent skylight volume
C   Plywood ribs
D   PTD finish plywood
E   Finished corner bead between materials
F   Insulated ceiling cavity at R-38 encapsulated
     fiberglass batt insulation
G   Vapor Diffusion Retarder (VDR)
H   Vertical corrugated 16 ounces copper
I   Housewrap
J   5/8 inches CDX exterior plywood sheathing
K   Insulated cavity at R-21 with encapsulated
     batt insul.
L   VDR with perm rating of 1.0 or less at warm
     side
M   Continuous two-part copper termite/base
     flashing, pressure treated sill plate on
     continuous foam sill seal
N   Foundation wall drainage plane
O   Flat roof areas fully soldered flast seam
     copper roofing with continuous ice and water
     shield on sheathing below
P   Standing seam copper roofing
Q   Fixed skylight: copper flashing as required
R   Ptd. GWB
S   Pittcon Z reveal
T   PTD wood base, flush with finished GWB
U   Finished floor
V   ¾ inches Subfloor
W   VIEGA "Climate Trak" two per cavity with
     PEX radiant floor tubing
X   R 30 Foil faced fiberglass batt insulation

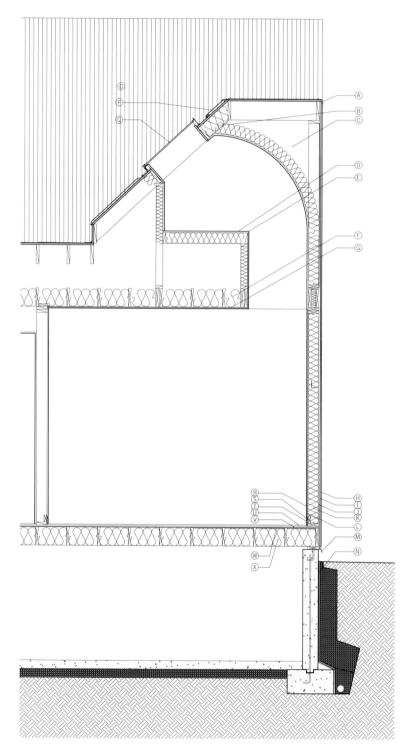

left top: Sun path and daylight diagram

left bottom: Master bedroom

right top: Dining room detail

right bottom: Guest bedroom

overleaf: South facade

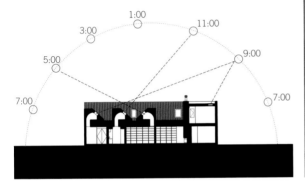

23 Beekman Place

Built in 1978, Paul Rudolph's penthouse apartment is an architectural icon for demonstrating his distinctive ideas about form, materials, and lifestyle. Until his death in 1997, Rudolph maintained the apartment as an ongoing experiment. Acting on his fascination with "the whole idea of [an] uncompleted building which is going to be expanded in unknown ways," he ceaselessly revised and altered the design as his needs and ideas changed, relocating millwork, plumbing fixtures, stairways, and even structural steel. Ultimately, he created multiple series of projects in one home, some of them temporary.

After Rudolph died, the apartment passed through several hands, and subsequent owners took up his tradition of experimentation, fitting aspects of the building to their needs. Its occupants struggled at times to address the legacy of Rudolph's impractical designs. Due to the overwhelming complexity of the original layout, not all of the renovations provided resolution.

Given the lack of a single historic design and our client's desire to modernize the apartment, we found ourselves charged with creating a more contemporary offspring of Rudolph's multifarious designs. This approach required in-depth documentation of the current and past states of the apartment, as well as a rigorous historical understanding of Rudolph's design principles, in order to imagine how he might have expanded his earlier experiments, given today's innovations and new technologies. Our role was that of contemporary architects seeking to implement the latest techniques and materials and that of archaeologists sorting through layers of the site, uncovering its history. We worked on this project in two ways, on site and virtually. Extensive computer modeling was used to gain a better understanding of the apartment's spatial complexity. The space, multilayered and confusing, couldn't be studied

Site section, looking north

Restored exterior

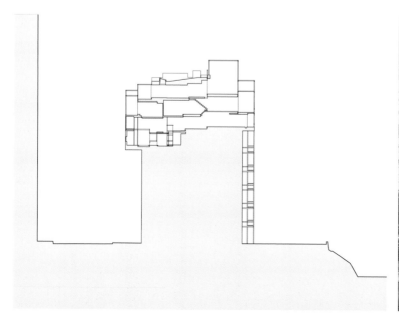

in physical fashion, other than through site visits. Orthographic architectural drawings, insufficient on their own as design tools, were supplemented by digital models for examining the spatial rigor of Rudolph's creation, in detail. For the first time, physical models were not used in any fashion by our studio.

After nearly thirty years of weathering and general wear, the apartment required major restoration work. Certain exterior details had resulted in severe water penetration and damage, requiring immediate remediation of the structure. New technologies and materials presented opportunities for making details visually identical to Rudolph's designs but functionally improved. Additionally, interior furnishings had begun to show their age. Many of the original acrylics and plastic laminates that Rudolph had used were not meant to last forever. Part of our work involved restoring salvageable elements, such as the acrylic floors, while replacing others with more durable alternatives.

Significant demolition had occurred within the apartment when we began work on the project. With the exception of the structural steel, intermittent floor finishes, a fireplace, a handful of demising walls, and some decorative handrail work, most of Rudolph's original home had been discarded. Also, due to access constraints—a tiny elevator and cramped

Demolition conditions

///

Paul Rudolph's original living room

///

stairs were the only means—much of the work was fabricated off-site, carried into the apartment piece by piece, assembled and tweaked for the tight fit, and then disassembled and taken off-site for finishing before being redelivered and reassembled. The challenges of these construction methods reiterated several of Rudolph's generative tools—that assemblages and their articulation of parts makes for thoroughly complex architecture.

One might expect any renovation to remain at odds with an architecture so detailed and all encompassing, yet Rudolph's legacy has thrived under these circumstances. That his original framework proved so flexible and resilient is one of the most compelling features of his work. Traces of former incarnations, present on the surface and hidden in the walls, are essential to the spirit of his architecture. This project demonstrates the problems and possibilities inherent in keeping modern architectural treasures both functional and vital while also preserving their character and significance.

Demolition conditions

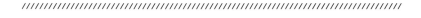

Detail of Paul Rudolph's original apartment

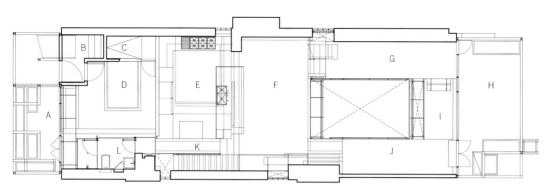

A	West Terrace	E	Kitchen	I	Balcony	H	Corridor
B	Public Corridor	F	Dining Area	J	Balcony	I	Entry
C	Closet	G	Balcony	K	Corridor	J	Bathroom
D	Bedroom	H	East Terrace	L	Bathroom		

A West Terrace   E Kitchen   I Balcony   H Corridor
B Public Corridor F Dining Area J Balcony I Entry
C Closet G Balcony K Corridor J Bathroom
D Bedroom H East Terrace L Bathroom

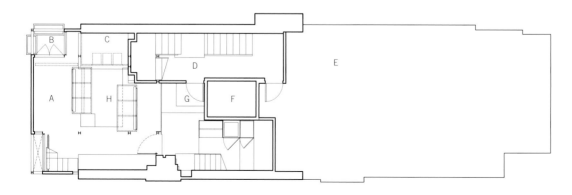

A Balcony   D Existing Elevator Control Room
B Study   E Sitting Area
C Existing Public   F Living Room
    Corridor   G East Terrace

A Study   E Adjacent Apartment
B West Terrace   F Existing Elevator Shaft
C Bedroom   G Entry
D Existing Public Corridor H Living Room

1'   5'   10'

///

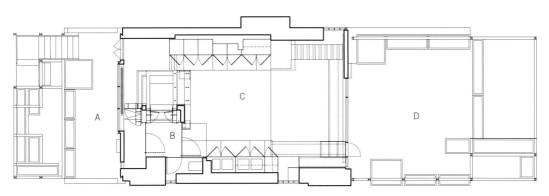

A   West Terrace
B   Master Bathroom
C   Master Bedroom
D   East Terrace

A	West Terrace	E	West Terrace	I	Balcony	M	Entry	Q	Study
B	Master Bathroom	F	Bedroom	J	East Terrace	N	Sitting Area	R	Living Room
C	Master Bedroom	G	Kitchen	K	Balcony	O	Living Room	S	Entry
D	East Terrace	H	Dining Area	L	Study	P	East Terrace		

top: Demolition conditions

center left: Main living area

center right: View from kitchen

bottom: Detail section at new handrail

///

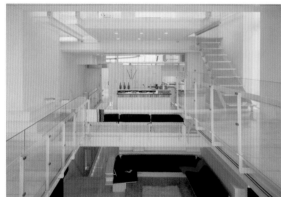

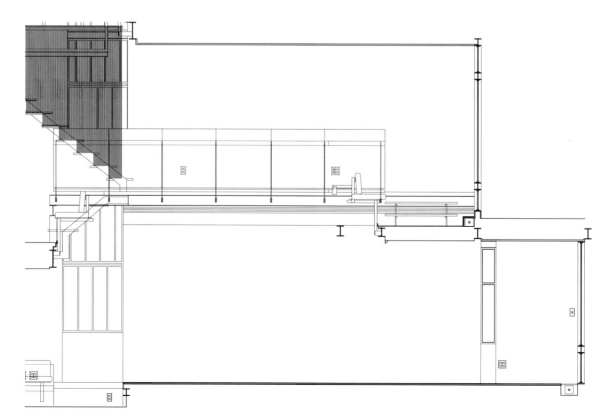

//

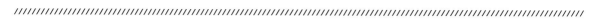

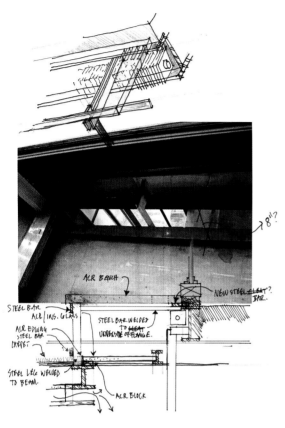

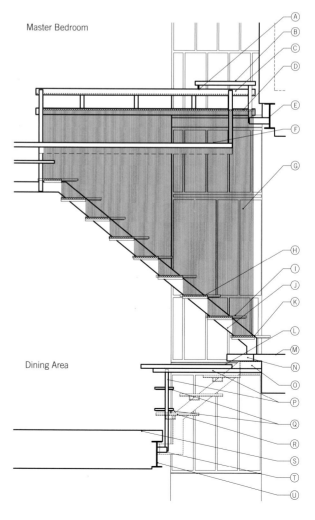

Master Bedroom

Dining Area

A   Outline of existing steel support for desk
B   Existing acrylic desk
C   Existing steel handrail assembly
D   New SS cap nuts, SS braided wire, and SS threaded
     rod at existing handrail holes
E   Existing steel beam
F   Existing floor
G   New continuous SS braided wire
H   New welded steel wire supports
I   Existing stair treads
J   Existing stair stringer
K   New SS cap nuts, SS braided wire, and SS bolt at
     steel handrail supports
L   New acrylic desk surface
M   Existing floor
N   New floor extension
O   New stringer extension
P   New steel bar support(s) for desk
Q   New steel flat support(s) welded to bard supports
     for shelves
R   Outline of existing stair treads
S   New floor
T   New steel cantilever supports welded to existing beam
U   Existing steel beam

top left: Study rendering

top right: New aircraft cable "rail" at folded
steel stair

bottom left: New construction and completed
restoration

bottom right: Office in Beekman Place
cantilever

//

//

//

A   1 ½" acrylic panel
B   Built-in bench assembly
C   Acrylic edging
D   Carpet on pad
E   Existing subfloor assembly
F   SS channel door guide with Teflon lining
      fastened to millwork column
G   Existing steel beam
H   New sprinkler pipe
I   Blocking glued to existing beam
J   Mirror on millwork panel
K   Plywood subpanel
L   Plywood finish layer
M   SS sill attached to underside of mirrored
      millwork panel
N   Plywood finish layer
O   Plywood sublayer
P   Steel supports beyond
Q   Door
R   Structural steel channel
S   New sprinkler head
T   SS shoe attached to glass panel, concealing
      sheave
U   Sheave
V   Sheave track
W   Wood block mortice to accept sheave track
      as required
X   SS angle fastened to plywood backer
Y   New sprinkler pipe
Z   Dashed lines indicate edges of existing steel
      column behind

a   New GWB ceiling
b   SS linear bar grille on HVAC diffuser assembly
c   Edge of millwork panel on HVAC diffuser assembly
d   Dashed lines indicate sprinkler riser in millwork column beyond
e   Electrical box for radiant floor thermostat
f   Electrical box for light switches mounted in south face of column
g   Sink filler body in millwork column
h   Faucet
i   Countertop
j   Silicon seal
k   Drip edge cut into countertop
l   Custom glass lavatory
m   Subcounter
n   Custom polished chrome trap
o   Rough plumbing buried in millwork column
p   Plywood finish layer
q   Plywood sublayer
r   Blocking fastened to stone floor
s   Dashed line indicates edge of existing steel column behind
t   Solid edging
u   Stone floor

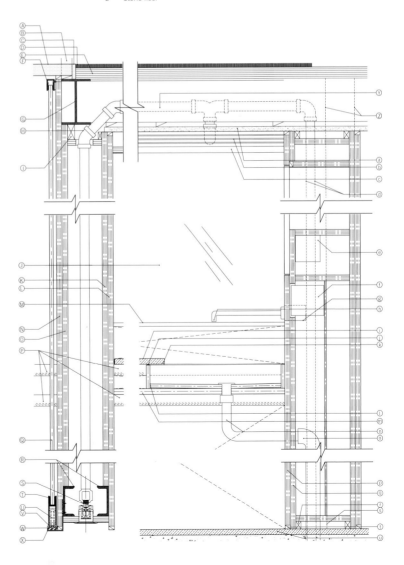

top: Restored original stairs and new shelf at master bedroom

bottom left: Master bedroom and bathroom

bottom right: New kitchen

Make Your Own Luck

Jared Della Valle and Andy Bernheimer joke about almost missing the deadline to submit their entry for the San Francisco Federal Courthouse Plaza competition. Their entry won the San Francisco commission, however, and once they learned the project would be built, they were obligated to form their own firm. Were it not for Andy and Jared's stated agenda, it might be hard to characterize the practice they founded. Whereas other young architects set out to design, DB's ambition is to build. Easier said than done: they draw their inspiration equally from beautiful, ethereal imagery and the per-square-foot cost of materials. As a friend, collaborator, and peer, I have seen firsthand the qualities that brought DB to the forefront of New York City's young architects. Their practice is founded on the notion that anyone can invent their own opportunities, whether in architecture, product design, or real estate development. Through this unusual model, they have followed through with designs that are rigorous, inventive, compelling—and that also get built.

What I have experienced working with Jared and Andy is my best evidence yet that luck is both a talent and a skill. As entrepreneurs, they are continually questioning conventional models of doing business. As architects, they are always looking for better ways of practicing. Their design processes are energized by ongoing questioning; however, their messiness is not confusion. Jared and Andy have found ways of working together and with collaborators that have proven highly successful. They have also pursued different ways of generating architecture, one based on lyric ideas, another based on engagement with a project's practical constraints.

A transcript of a meeting with Andy and Jared would be telling. While not irreverent, their approach includes significant laughter, as questions are raised and answers suggested. They allow themselves to get angry and, most importantly, to disagree with each other. This is not a small thing; it's what makes for great design. Ideas and buildings rarely emerge from a seamless process of elaboration and development. Instead they come out of the rough friction of a design process in which hypothetical buildings are buffeted by discussion, drawing, and dissent. Their meetings are not calm. Arguments break out. These heated debates open the process to everyone. The trust that Andy and Jared extend toward each other is abundantly clear. In the end, they are self-effacing, working to align their solutions and details. Their level of comfort is indicative of the faith they share in each other, their staff, their collaborators, and in their inclusive design process that, in the end, benefits from as much input as possible. This open-minded culture, which is a natural extension of Andy and Jared's own personalities and partnership, is responsible for DB's exceptional results.

An extension of this trust can also be seen in Della Valle and Bernheimer's work with outside collaborators. They invite architects, craftspeople, and design professionals to join in their process, casually extending the status of full equals. Under such generous auspices, a design can grow in unexpected ways, exploring unanticipated possibilities. In working with Guy Nordenson to design Artreehoose's long-span plywood joist system, the house evolved to become exponentially richer, with closely spaced plywood ribs creating texture and depth. To design custom cabinets for the kitchens and bathrooms in their 459 West 18th and 245 Tenth high-rise projects, they reached out to RIFRA Milano, a family-run manufacturer. Working within the parameters of the company's standard production line, DB achieved a level of elegance not usually attained within the New York construction market for projects of this type. In their East New York housing project, Glenmore Gardens, they defied conventional expectations about low-income housing by inviting a number of architecture firms, Architecture Research Office (ARO) included, to work with them. The team worked within a set palette of materials and a shared language of detail that ensured cohesion but also allowed each architect to imbue their house with lively individuality. Jared and Andy conceived of the prospective owners as retroactive collaborators. The pride of a first-time homeowner, as they envisioned it, drove us to really imagine these homes, rather than just design them. No wonder the project received forty times as many applicants as there were houses available.

Nothing is impossible for Della Valle Bernheimer, because Jared and Andy appreciate the nature of limitations and understand constraints as opportunities. For instance, how do you put a tower on a tiny, ill-shaped through-block site? You don't. You create two tall buildings connected by a fifty-foot-wide corridor. This is DB's Hudson Yards Tower project—a mixed-use, half-million-square-foot building located on the east end of Midtown in Manhattan. They needed to create a sense of urbanism in a part of the city where the full context would not be realized for twenty years. Central to DB's practice is the vision through which they perceive challenges. Selecting the right opportunities and melding them into design strategies are part of their art. What they make of these opportunities is almost always transformational.

Each of their projects embodies an idea or a sequence of related ideas. In what ways could a house be like a tree canopy? Can the etymology of the word *pavilion* influence a design? Is it possible to generate an eleven-story building out of steam? These ideas are often poetic images that arise during the course of conversation and are then applied as descriptive tools to guide decision-making, from concept to detail. Rather than elevate these ideas to strict metaphorical levels, DB uses them to sustain and steer projects. They are part of the joy of working collectively, because they allow for multiple interpretations. If that house is a tree canopy, what is its structure? How do you make a steam cloud out of stainless steel? Ideas seed conversation within the team, inspiring design, fabrication, and construction. A conceptually driven process may seem at odds with the methodology of seizing opportunities latent in constraints, but DB sustains a healthy level of tension between these two methods, aligning them in unexpected ways. In the Artreehoose, for example, a tree canopy liberates the design from the constraints of the restricted building site, creating a perfect synthesis of idea and circumstance.

One finds a refreshing sense of conviction in Jared and Andy. At any impasse, they are able to draw or talk their way to a solution and shift the situation in their favor. Their ingenuity, however, is not limited to architecture. Charging themselves with a difficult agenda at the outset of their careers, they have created a practice that has not readily settled into a conventional template. In their openness and in the risks they assume, Della Valle Bernheimer demonstrates considerable courage and faith in the design process.

—Stephen Cassell and Adam Yarinsky, principals, Architecture Research Office

Hudson Yards: Migration

In nature, the specific timing and stimuli for mass migrations are often inexplicable. The sudden rise of a large flock of birds can be triggered by imperceptible occurrences. But can a building reflect the imminent?

While opportunities are apparently limitless in New York, land is not. The adoption of the Hudson Yards Zoning District marks the single largest and last opportunity to expand the Midtown area. Together with the extension of the number 7 train, the rail yards development, and the Jacob K. Javits Convention Center expansion, a slow migration in the Midtown district is underway. We developed two speculative proposals for the site. The first, called Migration, is a midblock tower incorporating a hotel and residential condominiums.

Sitting on an irregular midblock site, the mass of the building splits into two towers, responding to zoning constraints and to a bifurcated program. Inherent in the design is a sense of the "shifts" in program: transitions in form, population, and economics. The formation of two towers, one smaller, echoes the sheared movement of the site's footprint and mediates between the scale of the current context and that of the future development of the Hudson Yards District. The towers' masses, with party walls bounding the east and west walls of the site, recall the architecture of the United Nations on the East Side, bracketing the island with an evocation of a similarly slender form. With varying frontages on both Thirty-fifth and Thirty-sixth streets, the towers shift on the east-west city grid, creating a foreground and background, as well as a dialogue between the two towers. The core that connects the buildings encloses an interior courtyard and offers panoramic views toward the east. The connection between Thirty-fifth and Thirty-sixth streets is a fifty-foot-wide space, filled with a solid bar of vertical transportation that joins the towers. Hotel, condominium, and commercial lobbies overlap at the base of the building, reiterating the shifting geometries.

The facade of the tower, at 650 feet tall, considers two vital views and scales. First, it addresses the panorama of the skyline at the scale of the city. Second, it engages the pedestrian and occupant at the scale of the detail. The result is a building that reinvents the

"Murmur #1," photograph by Richard Barnes   Site plan

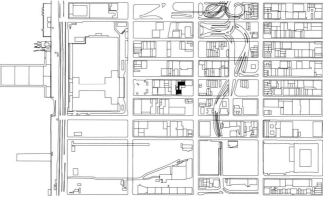

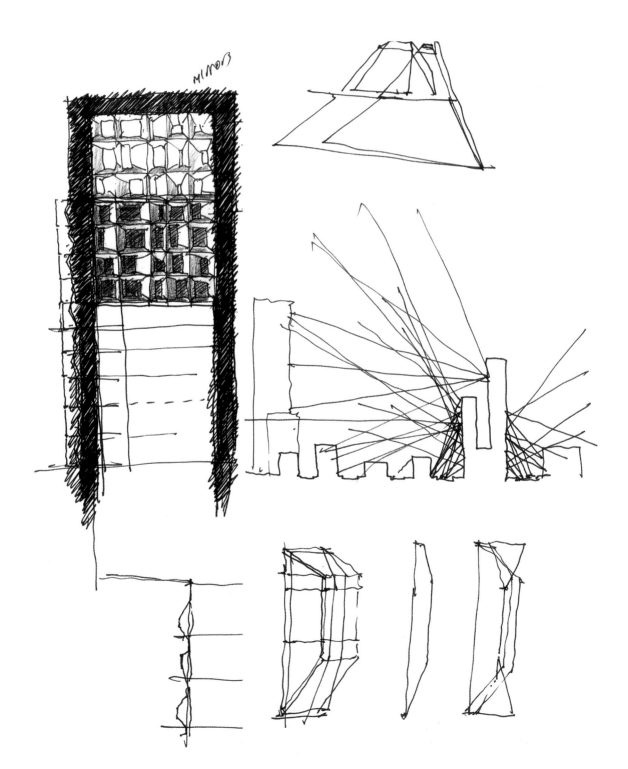

typical urban view through a manipulation of reflections. Facets or folds within the facade create fractured views. Economized through a unitized system, each panel is modular, the only difference from panel to panel being the location of the crease within a folded piece of glass. Shearing and folding conditions connect that which is separated: sky and street, north and south, front and back, top and bottom. Distorted images of the city and sky can be seen from a distance, while images not usually perceptible to pedestrians are brought down to street level. Simultaneously, this collection of units becomes a larger gesture within the city, a changing reflection of the neighborhood, an edifice that appears and disappears throughout the ever-changing performance of urban activity.

Modular facade studies

//

114   **top left:** Initial abstractions of Richard Barnes's "Murmur" photographs, transformed into facade patterns

top and center right: Facade studies

bottom: Study model

//

//

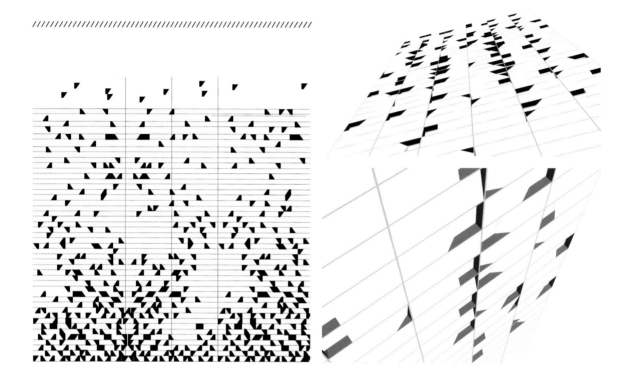

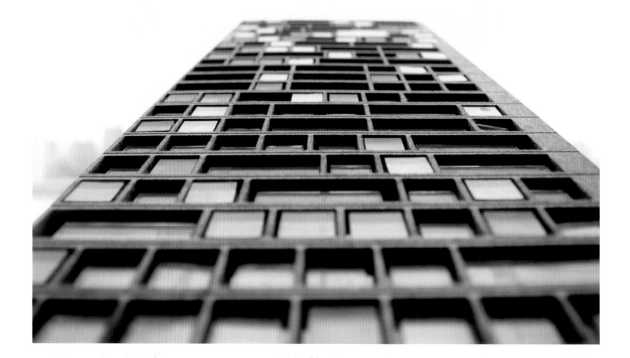

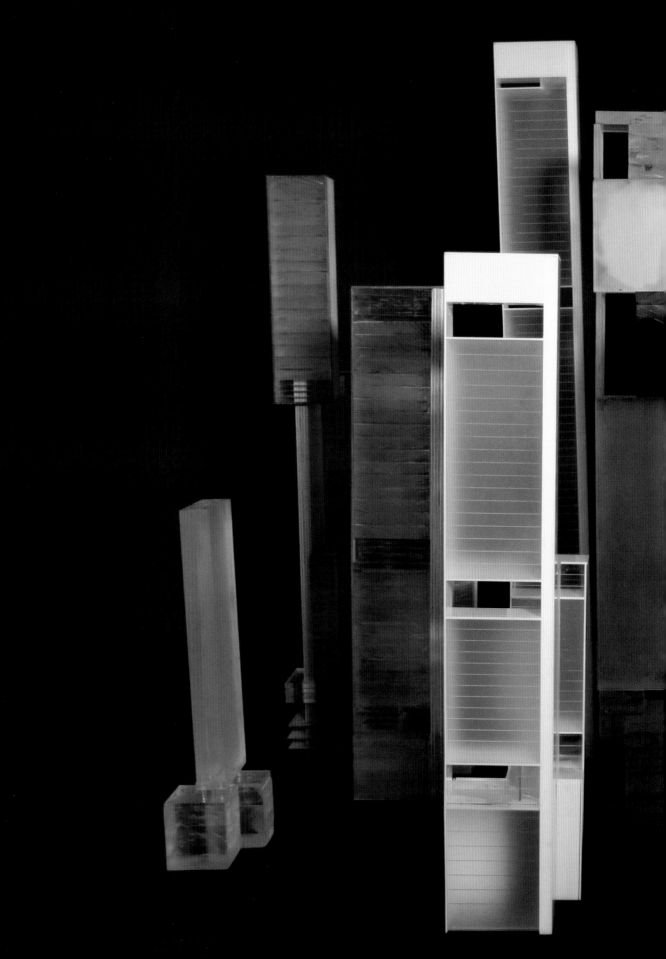

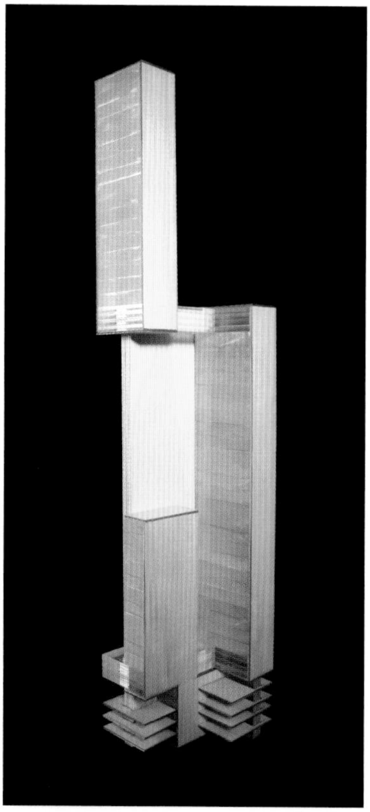
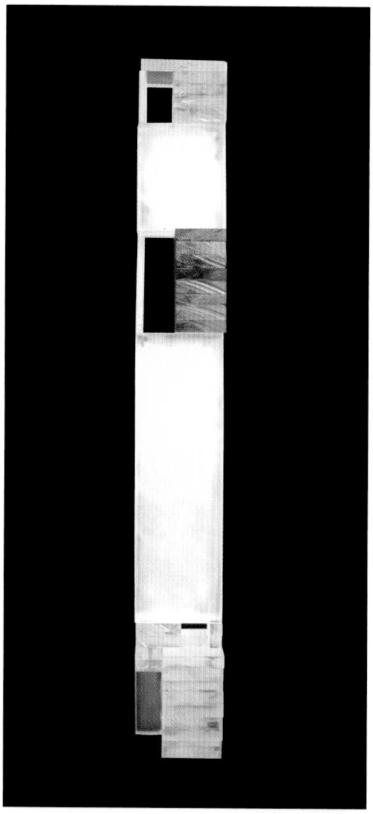
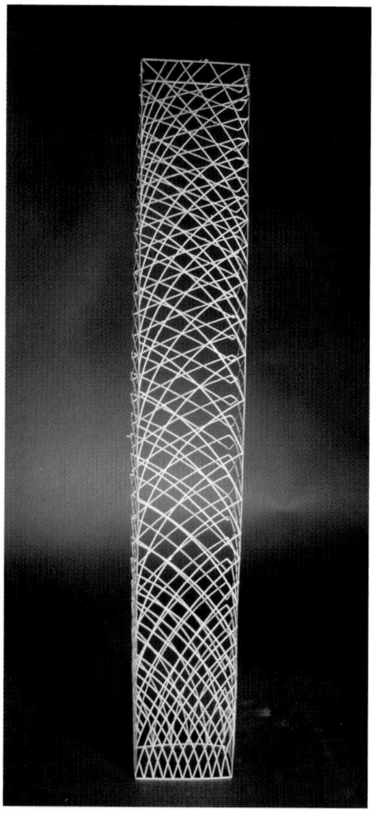
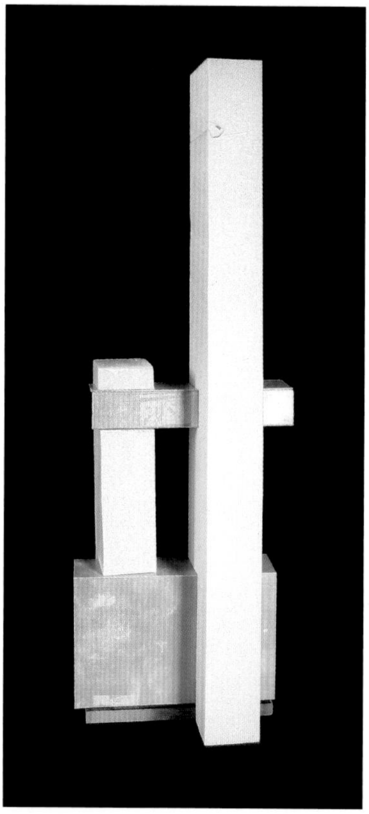
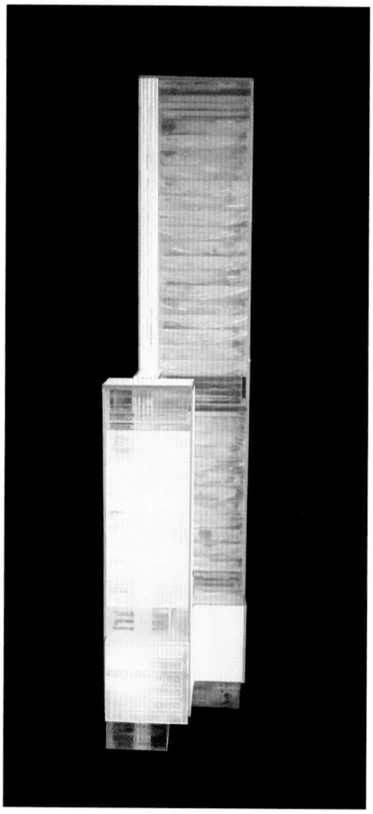
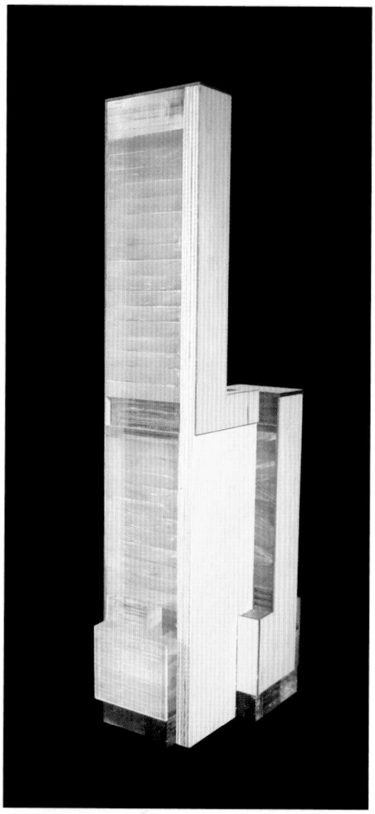

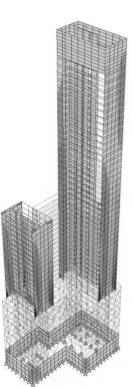

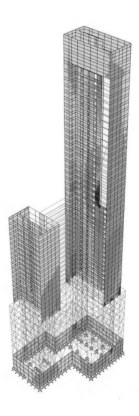

top left: Typical hotel plan

bottom left: Ground-floor plan

top right: Typical residential floor plan

bottom right: Lobby plan

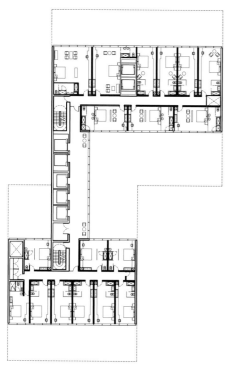

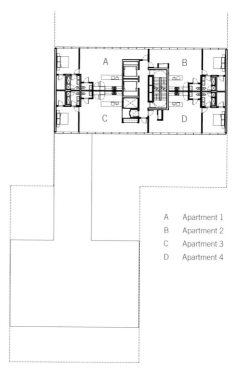

A   Apartment 1
B   Apartment 2
C   Apartment 3
D   Apartment 4

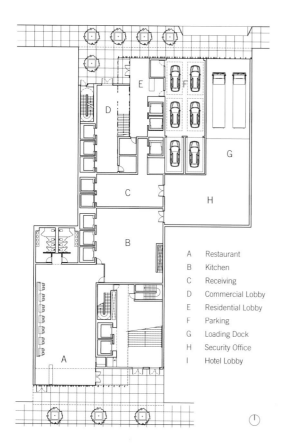

A   Restaurant
B   Kitchen
C   Receiving
D   Commercial Lobby
E   Residential Lobby
F   Parking
G   Loading Dock
H   Security Office
I   Hotel Lobby

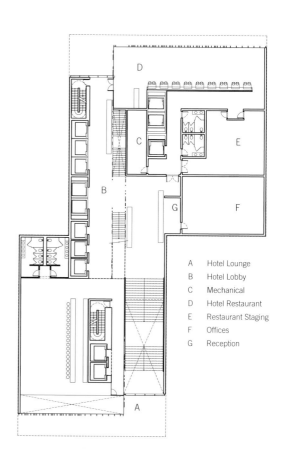

A   Hotel Lounge
B   Hotel Lobby
C   Mechanical
D   Hotel Restaurant
E   Restaurant Staging
F   Offices
G   Reception

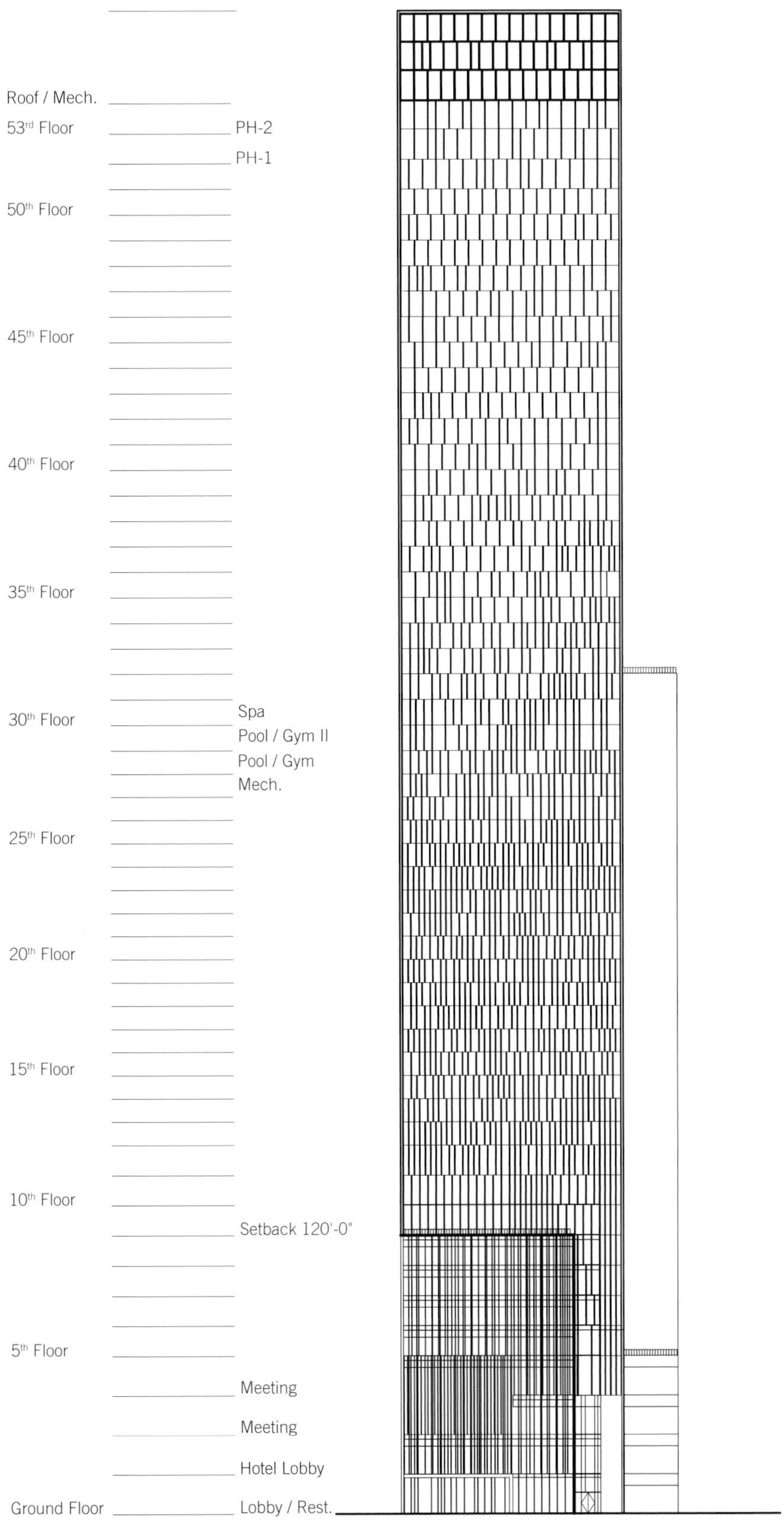

Roof / Mech.
53rd Floor _____ PH-2
                _____ PH-1

50th Floor

45th Floor

40th Floor

35th Floor

30th Floor _____ Spa
                _____ Pool / Gym II
                _____ Pool / Gym
                _____ Mech.

25th Floor

20th Floor

15th Floor

10th Floor
                _____ Setback 120'-0"

5th Floor

                _____ Meeting

                _____ Meeting

                _____ Hotel Lobby

Ground Floor _____ Lobby / Rest.

Hudson Yards: Shifting

The site of 450 Hudson Boulevard measures approximately one acre. With a permissible Federal Acquisition Rating of twenty-four, it has one of the highest allowable densities within the zoning resolution of the City of New York. Our second proposal for the Hudson Yards site is an approximately 1.1-million-square-foot mixed-use building to be developed as an environmentally sensitive contemporary structure. The project has the potential to afford one or all of the following uses: Exclusive Class A office space with podium floor plates in excess of 46,000 rentable square feet, a boutique hotel, and high-end luxury condominium residences. Additionally, the lower floors can accommodate retail units, potential cultural facilities, or parking.

The shape of the building is derived from zoning constraints, as well as from anticipated development within the neighborhood and iconic views afforded to the upper floors. The project uses a technique of shifting as the basis for its urban strategy, its articulation of masses, and ultimately, its facade expression.

Urban Strategy

The shifting volumes of the building create a form that mediates between the scales of the neighborhood currently and that of the future development of the Hudson Yards District. While no height restriction exists, 450 Hudson Boulevard exercises restraint and illustrates its recognition that the neighborhood is in an initial state of change. This is achieved by maximizing the typical tower-floor plate, allowing for multiple tenant configurations per floor.

Mass

The formation of the tower—a playful interpretation of zoning requirements—reiterates the stepping planes of rooftops and creates an abstracted and compressed interpretation of the Manhattan skyline. The required setback transitions over the face of the building, resulting in unexpected view corridors and outdoor spaces.

Facade study

Site plan

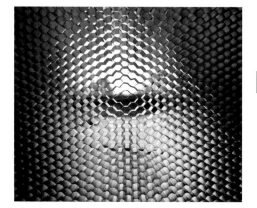

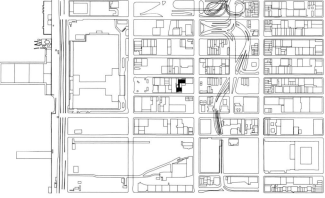

Facade

The facade at 450 Hudson Boulevard is the result of an investigation of texture, examined by shifting the position and spacing of mullions in relationship to glass panes and by a deliberate calibration of reflectivity across the facade. Standard five-foot mullion spacing creates static and repetitive frames of exterior views, but by varying the spacing, discrete moments occur along the cardinal views, associated with each face of the building. The glass's reflectivity also varies throughout the structure. Highly reflective curtain-wall glass mullions and soffits of the recessed areas are offset against the less reflective treatment of the building's dominant faces. This difference in reflectivity, along with the shifting of the mullions from inside to outside of the glass, modulates the facade and causes a visual inversion that effectively doubles the perception of the shift.

Program Strategy

The primary lobby of the office is accessed via the boulevard. A secondary, executive lobby is located on Thirty-fifth Street, just blocks from Penn Station. Retail spaces line the front of the boulevard and wrap around the corners of Thirty-fifth and Thirty-sixth streets. Access to parking and loading docks is available on Thirty-sixth Street. Below grade, there are three subfloors of retail, service, and parking; a connection to the midblock garage is to be built underneath the boulevard.

The building podium occupies the full allowable lot and rises to a height of 120 feet. Floors one through eight contain retail units, ground-floor services, and six floors of commercial offices totaling more than 45,500 rentable square feet per floor (an area large enough to accommodate trading floors). A shifting setback, along three of the building's faces, provides over 25,000 square feet of outdoor space and a greater than usual number of corner offices. The typical plates, for floors nine through thirty-three, amount to approximately 33,000 rentable square feet. A compact core at the center of each floor allows for multiple configurations.

View Corridors

Due to the shift in plan, the building design is able to break away from the conventional one-view-per-side alignment employed by most towers. Instead, the cardinal view of each face is pulled further into the building, affording a diversity of views along all four facades . Also, at less than five stories, the current street height in the area is relatively low. For this reason, the views from 450 Hudson are extensive in all directions, beginning in the upper floors of the podium. Even as the neighborhood continues to develop, the view to the east—of Midtown Manhattan and the Empire State Building—will be preserved, due to the adjacent landmarked context.

Green roofs and terraces will reduce the heat island effect, filter storm water, improve air quality, and provide increased vegetation. In areas with limited access, low-maintenance extensive green roof systems will be used. In heavily trafficked areas, deeper and more intensive roofs will be implemented, which will facilitate the planting of more diverse vegetation.

The results of these strategies will include reduced operating costs and relieved demand on the city's resources, but more vitally, these improvements will enhance the experiences of the people who live and work in and around the building.

//

top: Typical orthogonal plan, lengthened with additional cornering

center left: View maximization diagram

center right: Reinterpretation of existing zoning restrictions

bottom: Context rendering

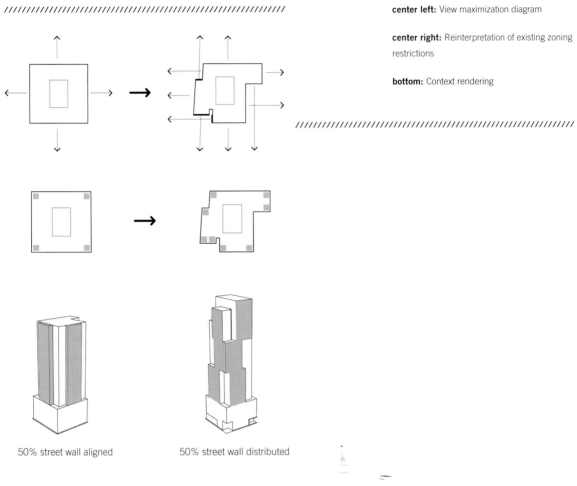

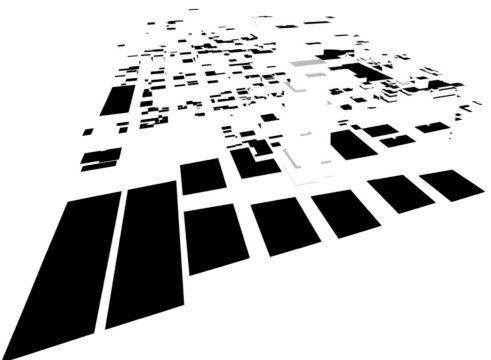

50% street wall aligned   50% street wall distributed

top left: Programming diagram

top right: Hudson Yards Towers II aerial

bottom: West elevation and height comparison

//

//

LEGEND

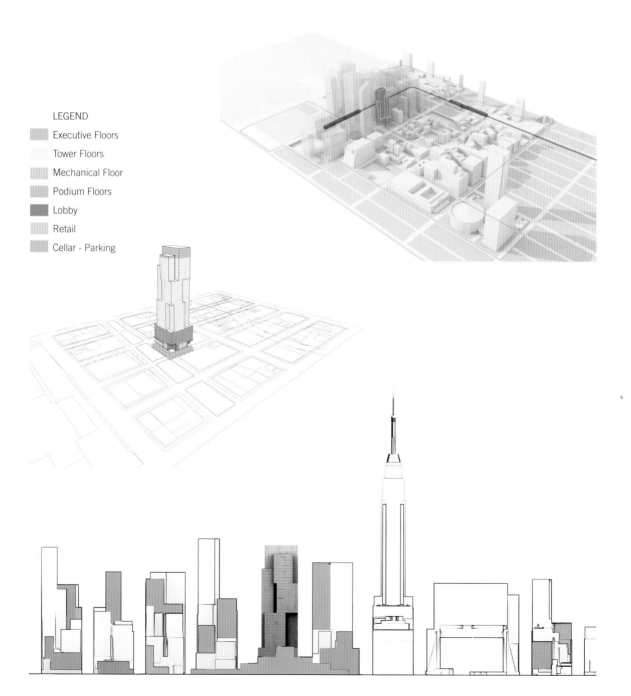

Executive Floors

Tower Floors

Mechanical Floor

Podium Floors

Lobby

Retail

Cellar - Parking

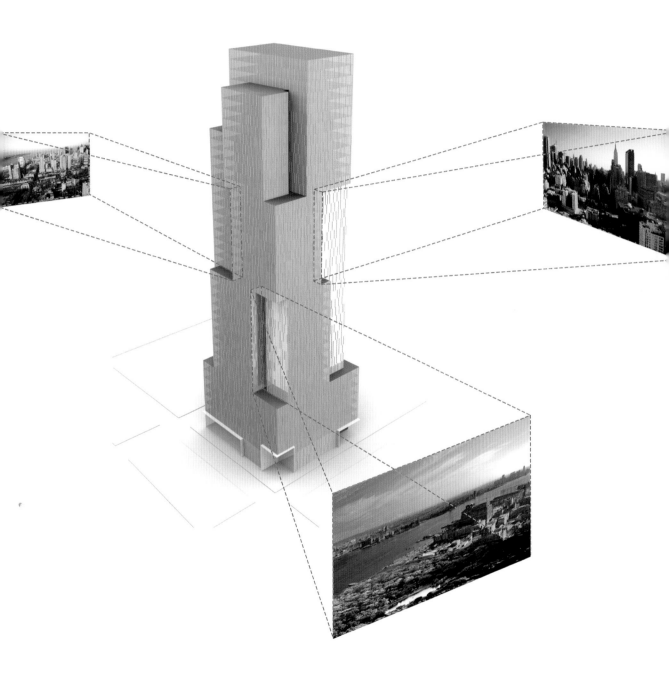

Aquacenter

Our proposal for the Aquacenter in Aalborg, Denmark, presents an image of people both walking on water and puncturing and possessing a transmutable volume. The building consolidates several swimming activities into one large, multifunctional pool. Unlike traditional facilities, where straight lines provide the vector of movement, this swimming complex imagines a circuit in which people can move in any direction, from use to use, while the depths of each area vary along an undulating surface, unified by a single, unbroken sheet of water.

Architecturally, this project heightens one's visual cognizance of thickness and thinness. One enters the building from beneath the water's surface; the pool's undulating shapes create an impression of shelter within the entryway, locker room, and spa. Thus the topography defines the character and quality of the spaces. Once a swimmer has changed and readied for activity, he or she gains access to the pool by way of stairs, ascending into an area that is surrounded on all sides by water. This sequence is followed by an act of resurfacing prior to the point of immersion. Swimmers can see others, seemingly walking on a liquid surface. Because in some areas, the walkable surface is centimeters below water level, users illogically appear to float. This is a subversion of the normative expectation that water is unstable and uniformly penetrable.

The swimming center occupying the second floor of the structure reconnects to the landscape through massive expanses of glass. Sandwiched between two solid surfaces of textured metal paneling, the glass box of the pool reestablishes a horizon line above the ground, giving those who are swimming a sense that they are hovering above the landscape. Continually subverting a sense of in and out, up and down, large glass panels slide apart to connect an outdoor swimming area with the main interior space. A translucent glass ceiling casts a diffuse glow on the interior, like that of a thin cloudcover illuminated by the sun.

Conceptual collage

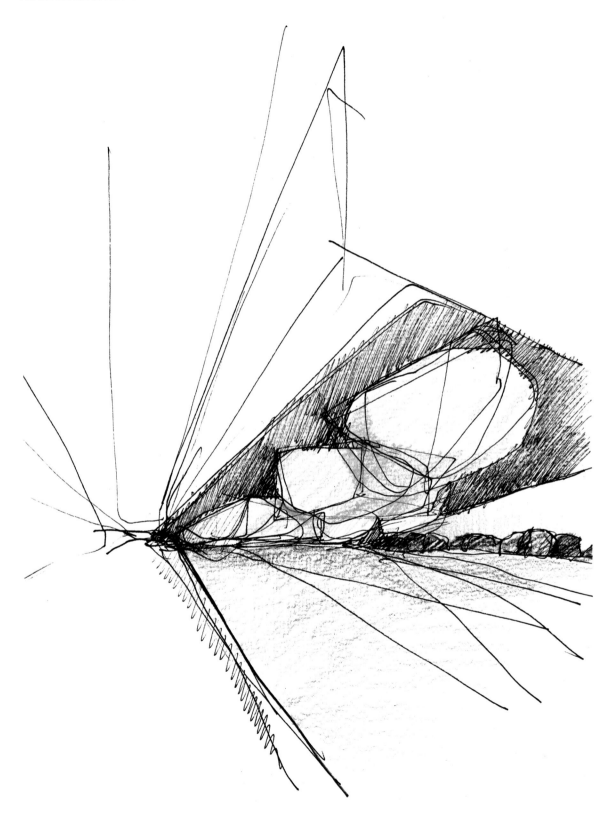

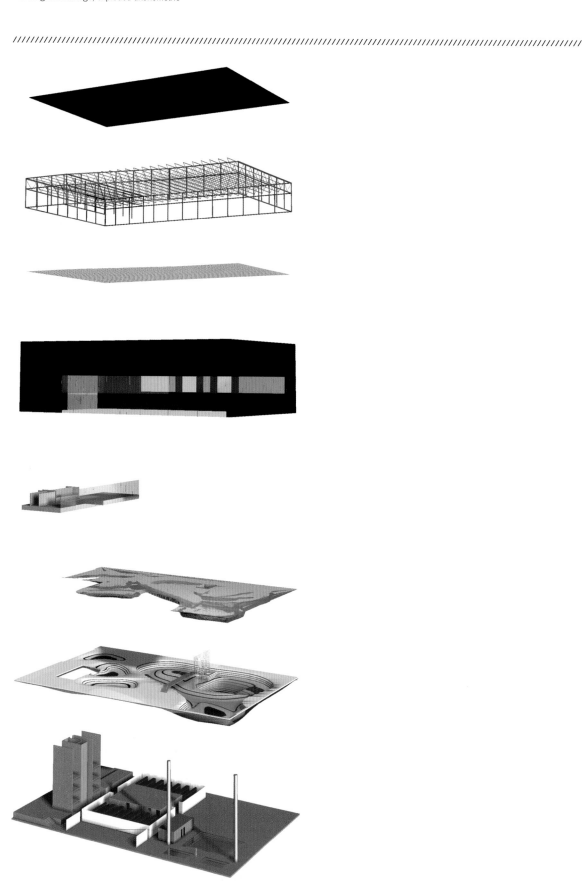

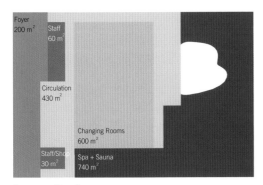

Program allocation

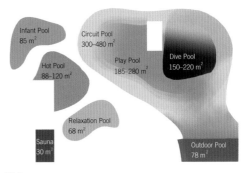

Water

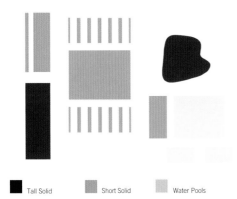

Solid volumes

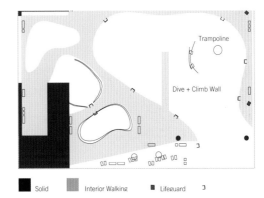

Recreational areas

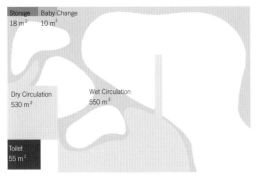

Circulation

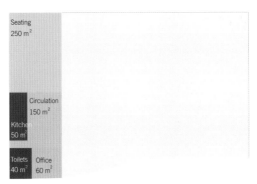

Amenities

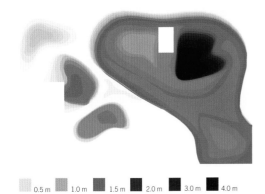

Pool depth

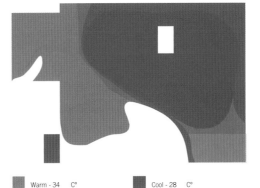

Pool temperature

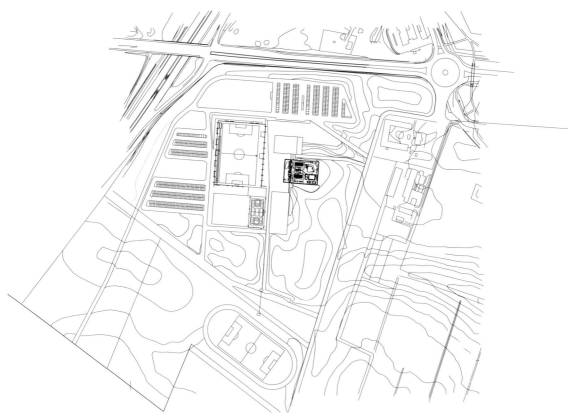

A	Vestibule	D	Wading Pool
B	Diving Board	E	Restroom
C	Deep Pool	F	Restroom

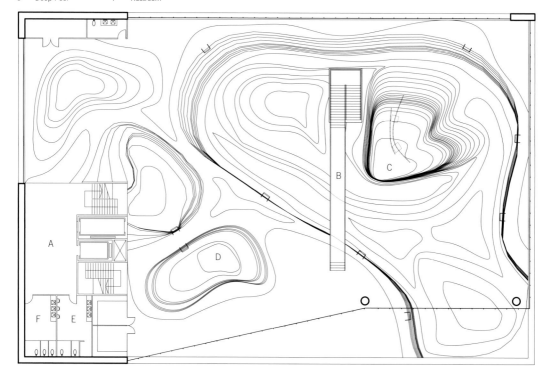

//

A　Vestibule
B　Restroom
C　Restroom

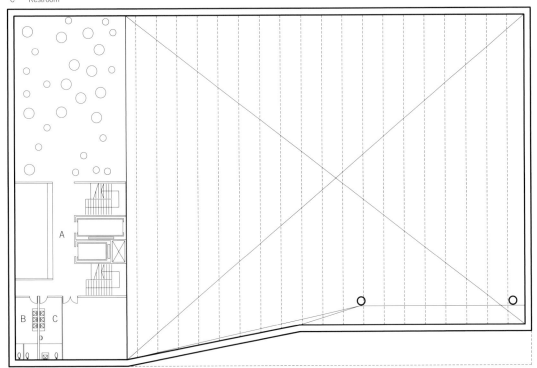

A　Cafe　　　　　　C　Locker Room
B　Locker Room　　　D　Vestibule

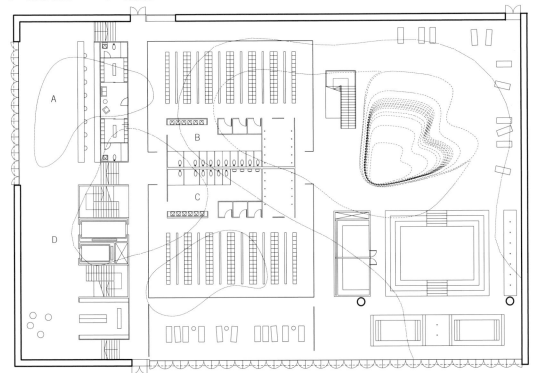

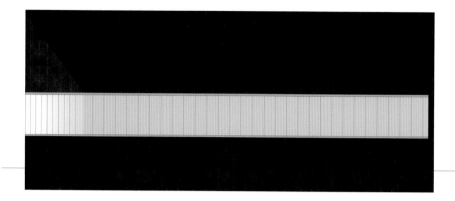

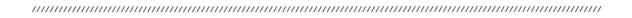

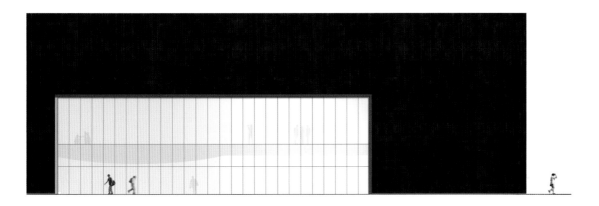

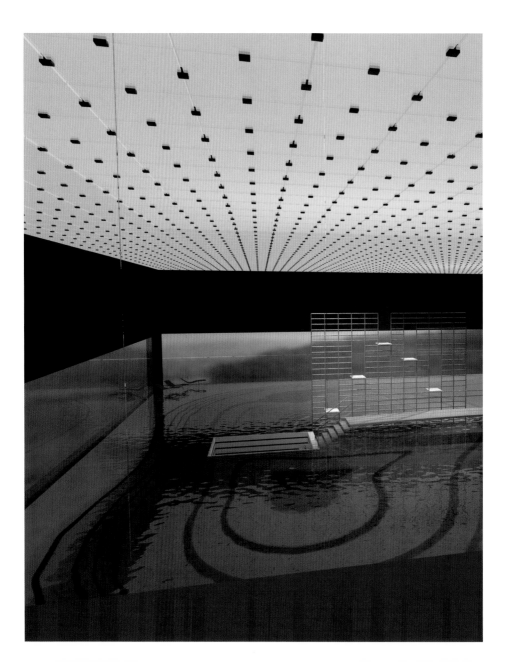

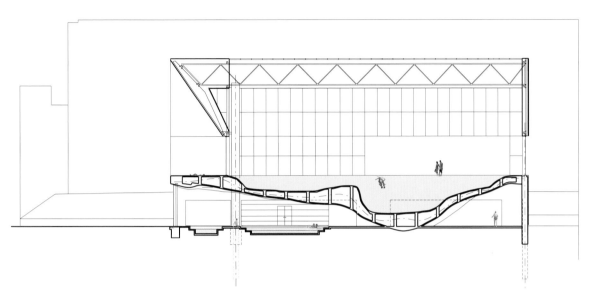

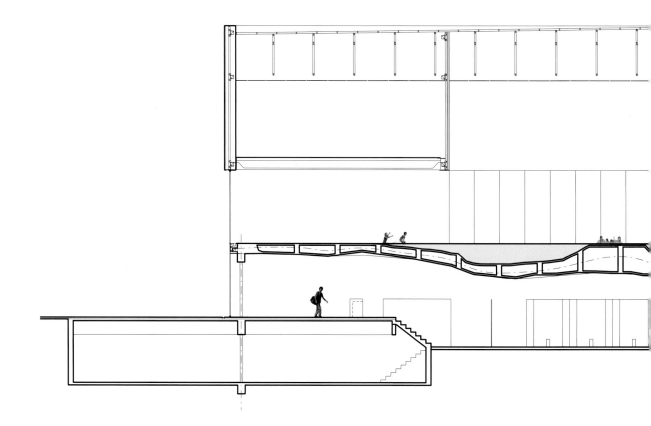

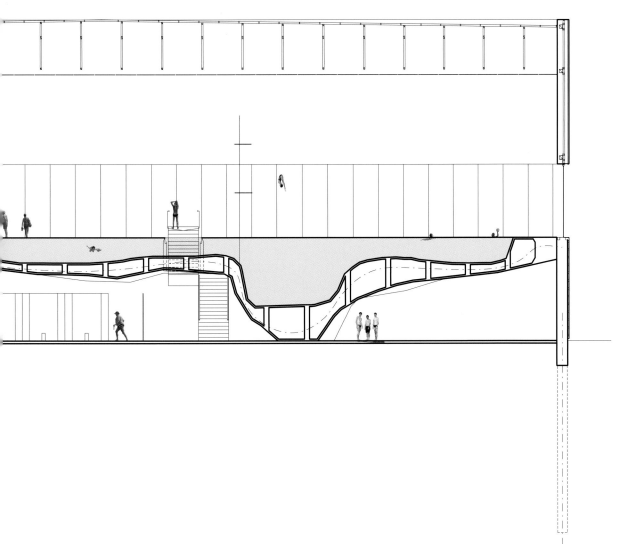

450 Golden Gate Plaza

I…want you to consider the opposite of what you do by definition—not only to construct buildings, but to create open space to preserve emptiness, so that we are not only faced with *fullness*, but have the emptiness in which to repose.

—Wim Wenders[1]

The redesign of the plaza at 450 Golden Gate Avenue accommodates a diverse series of activities. It is responsible for presenting a clear and safe path for all types of pedestrian traffic. It provides safe spaces, acting as a buffer between the street and the Burton Building, and it projects an image of strength, in material and spirit.

The design for the renovation of the Federal Plaza in San Francisco (the original plaza was built in the early 1960s and closed in the late '80s) was awarded through an open international design competition. Our entry answered a demand in the brief to address issues of wind, light, occupancy, and the "poetics of security," as it was termed. Working at an urban scale—the site is 125 feet wide by 400 feet long—it was imperative that we invent a tool for transforming a large-scale architectural action into an intimate setting. Our tool was a single line: an enormous tilted plane sloping from the low end of the site to the front of the building at the center of the plaza. This tilt continues to the opposite end of the site, rising a total of ten feet above the existing grade. Because of the length of the site, all code issues became nonfactors. The slope increases gradually, and landings and handrails become unnecessary. In this way, the stigma of separate entry means for the disabled is avoided, and a democratization of access is achieved. All traffic uses the same path of travel. This line also became a generative tool for reducing the scale of the immense site; additional intermittent folds and tilts were used for light fixtures, seating areas, and planters for flowers, grasses, and trees.

Invited by the General Services Administration several years later, DB proposed additional interventions for the plaza. These included a canopy structure at the west end. Like a cloud disappearing into the sky, it was envisioned as a lattice of stainless steel framing elements that diffuse daylight, cast interesting shadows, and act as light fixtures at night. Though made of metal, the transparency of this assemblage would bring lightness to the overall structure, adding intimacy and shelter to the raised west end. This canopy could also act as a planting trellis, with vines growing amidst the metalwork.

Because the existing tree planters could not accommodate larger root structures, DB proposed using these wells for the artificial, trunklike structures of the canopy. Between these pieces, rectangular metal frames span from a low point near the west wall to a high point near the portico. Each frame is approximately three feet tall and tilts slightly towards the east. In plan, the assemblage appears as a simple series of straight lines. In section, it appears as a tilted plane. The canopy structure could also act as a spoiler (particularly if planted with vines), casting an eastward wind shadow across the plaza.

1. Quoted from "The Urban Landscape from the Point of View of Images" in Wim Wenders, *The Act of Seeing: Essays and Conversations*, trans. Michael Hofmann (London and Boston: Faber and Faber, 1997), 101.

///

top left: Design sketch

top right: Section at raised west end

bottom: Night view at Golden Gate Avenue
entry

//

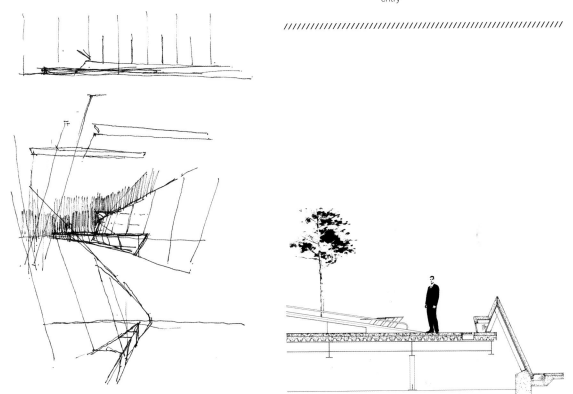

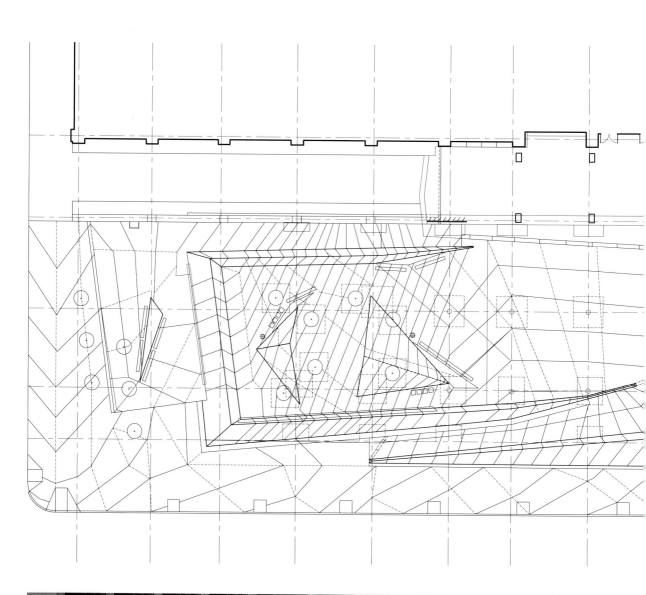

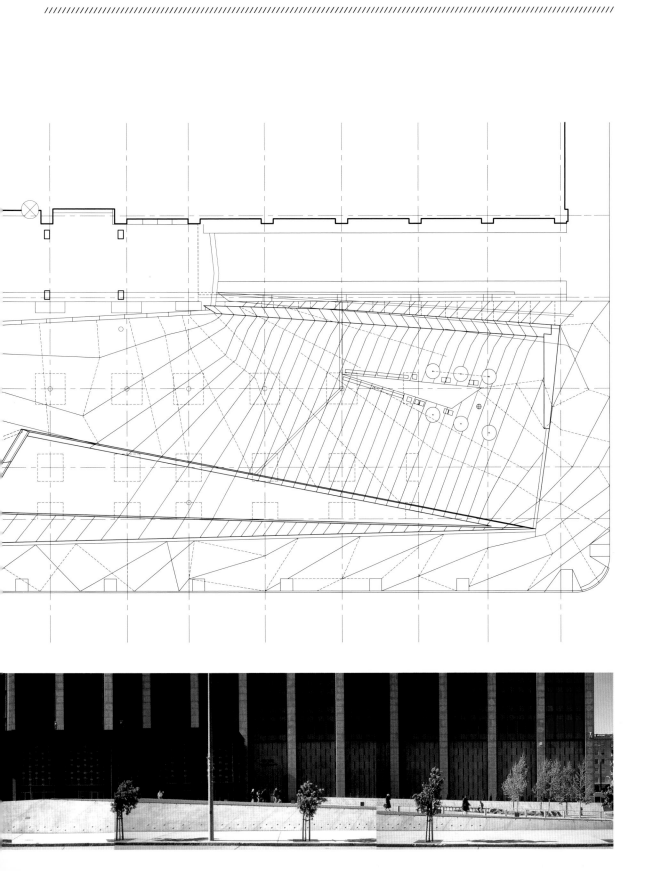

//

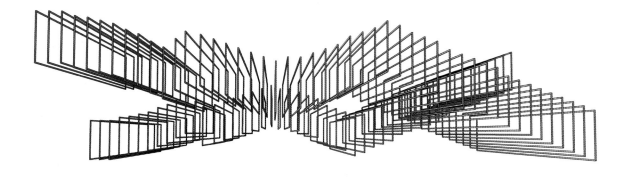

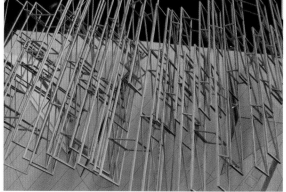

top left and right: Study models

bottom: Night view of canopy

overleaf: Steel-frame canopy

//

//

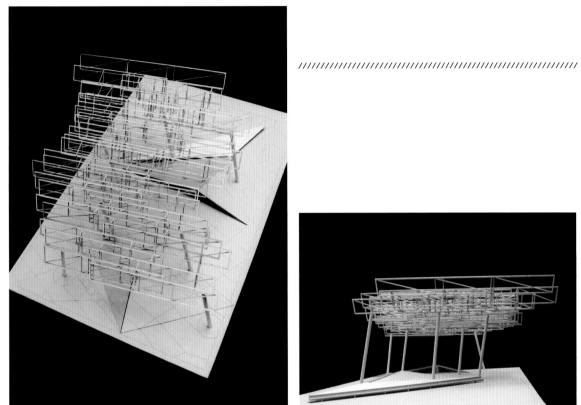

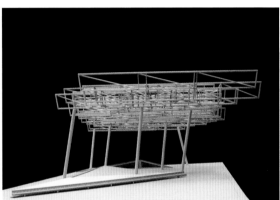

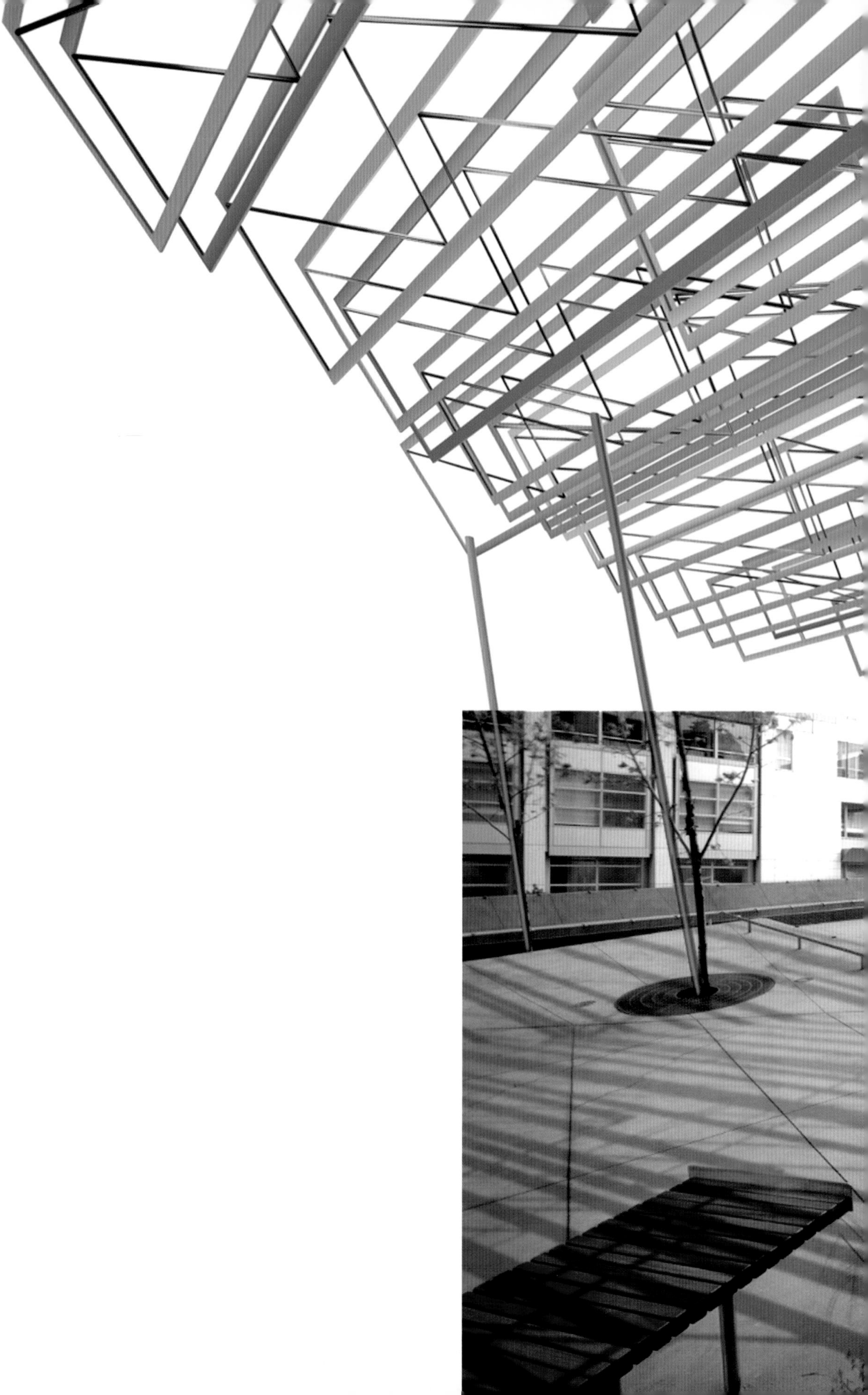

Glenmore Gardens

Modern row-house construction within New York City's affordable housing typology has typically offered little house-to-house differentiation and therefore little opportunity for architecture to create a clear sense of identity or individuation. A first home purchase—a milestone in anyone's lifetime—signifies the act of taking stake in a community. The project, which our firm developed, planned, and codesigned, introduced ten affordable homes within five semidetached buildings in East New York, Brooklyn.

In spirit, this project engages architecture in a manner similar to the Weißenhofsiedlung in Stuttgart, Germany, however, in more pragmatic economic terms. It is not an exhibition about a grandiose concept of new architecture but a collection of small-scale ideas magnified through a variety of deployments by several young architects seeking collaboratively to imbue a humble housing type with dignity. This project engages the basic need for affordable housing within the realms of aesthetics, economics, and politics.

Acting as both developer and architect, our firm coordinated the design and construction of these homes as a part of the New Foundations program for the NYC Department of Housing Preservation and Development. This program allows for land generating little or no tax revenue to be transferred to private developers, who must adhere to certain stipulations and standards describing what can be built and how. The program's typical subscribers are developer-contractors, firms that can finance, design, and build homes under one imprimatur. This eliminates any likelihood that architects would be granted a voice in the process, as our profession is stereotypically seen as an impediment to efficient, cost-effective design. We responded to this program—along with Architecture Research Office, Briggs Knowles Architecture + Design, and Lewis.Tsurumaki.Lewis—with the intention of challenging such stereotypes.

Via a charrette process, the four firms developed two housing types that mimic the local architectural language: a slab-on-grade, three-story structure and a two-story building with subgrade floors and a stoop entry. Simultaneously, we developed a palette of materials to be shared across the five buildings. Each architecture firm had full latitude in the deployment of these materials to create unique exterior compositions. Standardized details were developed for all houses, and the architects shared these details within their differentiated compositions in order to reduce costs and control the quality and consistency of construction.

In the two buildings designed by DB, we signified difference through either a directional shift in a common material or an explicit change in the type of cladding. In the DB 1 building, the primary cladding material is recycled aluminum; it shifts ninety degrees along the party wall of two semidetached homes. This simple directional change creates an identifiable difference through light and color transitions. Though the primary material remains consistent over the bulk of the building, the rotation causes the aluminum to appear both dark and light, gray or white, depending on the time of day and type of light. In our second DB building, a cedar box embeds itself within a corrugated aluminum shell at the second floor. This wooden object distinguishes the homeowner's territory from the first-floor rental unit.

///

///

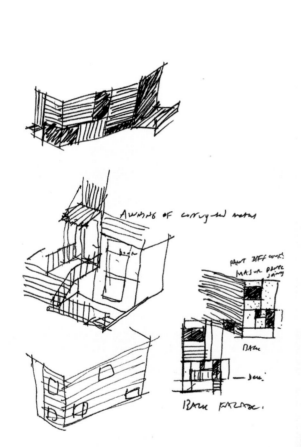

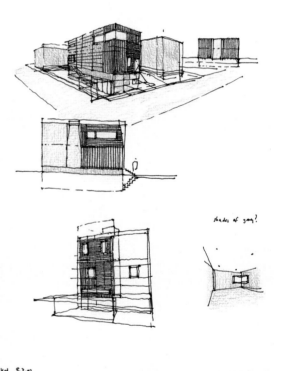

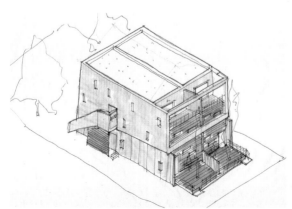

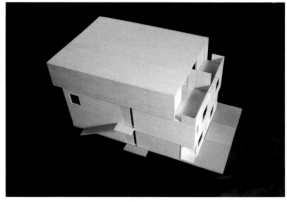

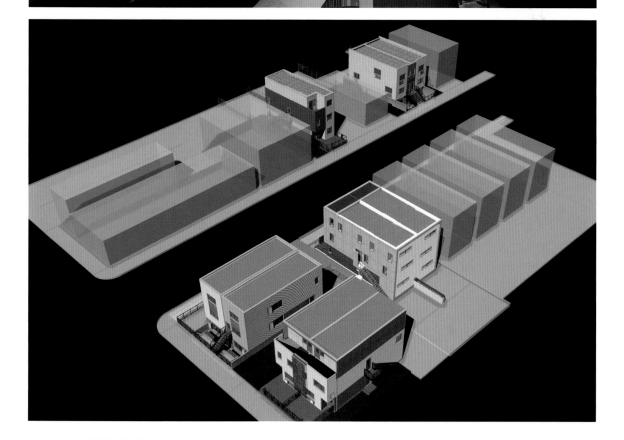

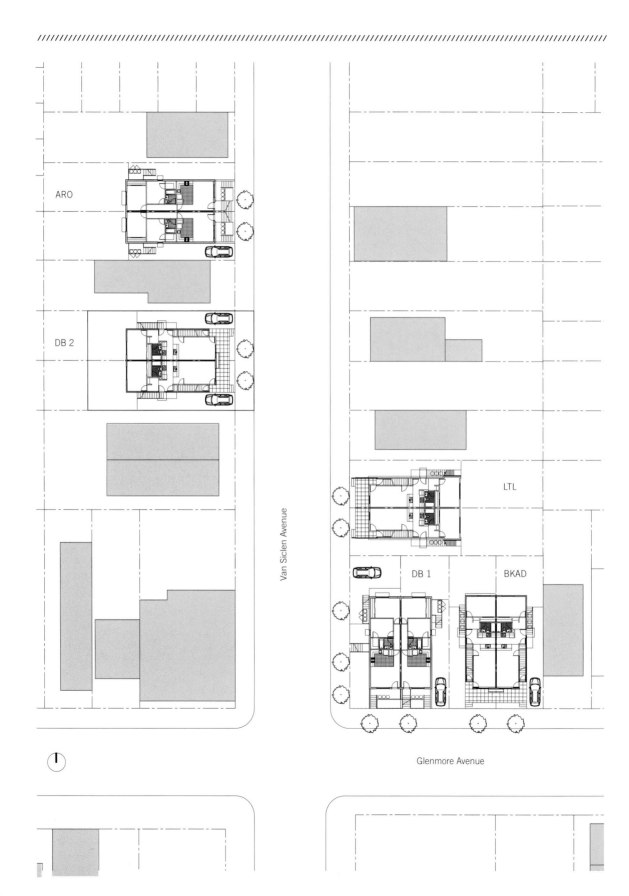

ARO

DB 2

Van Siclen Avenue

LTL

DB 1

BKAD

Glenmore Avenue

///

top, left to right:

Slab-on-grade building type:

Ground-floor plan

Second-floor plan

Third-floor plan

bottom: DB 2

//

A	Garden	A	Bedroom	A	Bedroom
B	Bedroom	B	Bathroom	B	Bathroom
C	Bathroom	C	Kitchen	C	Bedroom
D	Kitchen	D	Living Room		
E	Living Room				

///

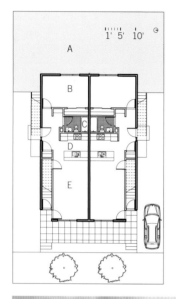

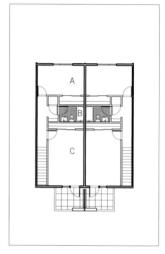

top, left to right:

Raised stoop building type:

Basement plan

Ground-floor plan

Second floor plan

bottom: DB 2, ARO

///

A	Bedroom	A	Parking	A	Bedroom
B	Office	B	Kitchen	B	Bathroom
C	Bathroom	C	Laundry	C	Bedroom
D	Kitchen	D	Bathroom	D	Bedroom
E	Living Room	E	Living Room		

///

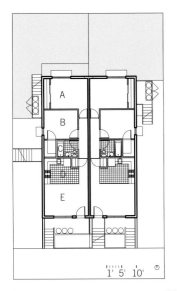
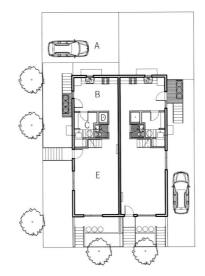
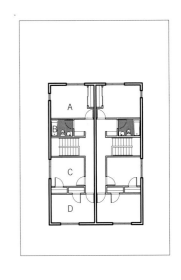

New owners who took possession in 2007 as part of the New Foundations program, run by the NYC Department of Housing Preservation and Development.

//

//

Project Index

Centering the Civic

San Francisco Museum of Art, 1996

team: Jared Della Valle and Andrew Bernheimer

A series of digital photo-collages showing how city surfaces are papered with documents that question the impact of collective action in urban spaces.

//

450 Golden Gate Plaza

San Francisco, Calif., 1996–2000, (pp.148–159)

Winner, San Francisco Prize in Architecture, 1996

area: 45,000 sq. ft.
team: Jared Della Valle and Andrew Bernheimer
architect of record: Del Campo and Maru

A folded surface acts to reduce the scale of an immense site. Large and small tilts and creases in a vast horizontal surface form a ramp that provides all citizens with equal access to the courthouse. Smaller folds are used as locations for light fixtures, seating areas, and planters for flowers, grasses, and trees.

Loft

New York, N.Y., 1998–99

area: 1,700 sq. ft.
team: Jared Della Valle and Andrew Bernheimer
contractor: David Kelleran

A solitary box treated with red-aniline dye conceals doors and moving walls and defines domestic spaces within an open industrial loft.

//

Artist's Loft

Boston, Mass., 1998–99

area: 2,200 sq. ft.

team: Jared Della Valle and Andrew Bernheimer

contractor: Fort Hill Construction

metalwork: Todrin Laser with Noubissi Boyques

Two walls made of laser-cut steel plates bow and flex as programmatic requirements grow or shrink. These walls separate a ceramics studio and bedroom suite from a central display area for the work of the artist. Nearly all panels pivot, allowing the space to expand and contract for gallery shows.

//

TKTS2K Competition

New York, N.Y., 1999

area: 800 sq. ft.

team: Jared Della Valle, Andrew Bernheimer, Paul Puciata, and Burck Schellenberg

An exterior skin fabricated of laser-cut pearwood veneer, laminated between sheets of glass, creates an unexpectedly tactile and durable piece of architecture. In this scheme for a new ticket booth in Times Square, the iconic TKTS logo is repeatedly removed from the veneer, forming the pattern of a larger supergraphic. Lighting placed between two layers of glass inside a prefabricated steel box causes the wood to glow and also illuminates the interior space of the booth.

//

Harvey Milk Plaza

San Francisco, Calif., 2000

team: Jared Della Valle, Andrew Bernheimer, Burck Schellenberg, and
    Jason Jimenez

The existing streetscape within a defined competition zone is resurfaced with white stone, and all surrounding buildings are painted white, exposing a vibrant community of people and activity. In daylight, this new surface receives sun, shadows, and natural reflections. At night, pendant lights hang from existing tension wires, and glowing bench and curb lights illuminate the street and its surroundings, kaleidoscopically altering a new landscape.

Loft

New York, N.Y., 2000–02

area: 2,100 sq. ft.
team: Jared Della Valle, Andrew Bernheimer, and Ryan Harasimowicz
contractor: Ian Banks

The central object of this triplex apartment is an ebonized oak-and-steel stair wrapped in Cocobolo wood. The kitchen and stairwell enclosures, fabricated from stainless steel and Cocobolo wood, respectively, appear as boxed insertions on the ground floor. This language is repeated in the master suite on the second floor, as similarly clad storage units protrude into the stairwell and define additional rooms.

/// ///

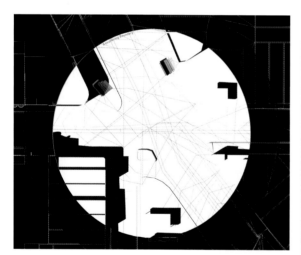

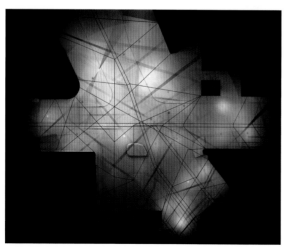

Loft

New York, N.Y., 2001–02

area: 1,400 sq. ft.

team: Jared Della Valle, Andrew Bernheimer

contractor: Richard Smith

Two sliding panels fabricated from air-entrained aluminum foam create an accessible and transformable apartment for twin brothers.

Loft

New York, N.Y., 2001–02

area: 1,700 sq. ft.

team: Jared Della Valle and Andrew Bernheimer

contractor: Richard Smith

//

L!brary

Staten Island, N.Y., 2000–02

Part of the Robin Hood Foundation's Public School Initiative

area: 2,000 sq.ft.

team: Jared Della Valle, Andrew Bernheimer, and George Dawes

contractor: AWL Contracting

Inserted into two previously underused classrooms, the new library at Public School 18, in the Brighton neighborhood of Staten Island, was designed to create three encounters. First, one encounters the stainless steel box, a gleaming metal object that occupies the space of the hallway and fosters curiosity. Appearing as a solid object accessible through two pivoting doors, it allows for glimpses of the activity inside, through windows located at child's eye level. Within the box, the second encounter is the compressed space, composed of book stacks filled with information. The third encounter is the laboratory, a lively colorful space where one may interface with gathered information. The library interior, bordered on one side by the stainless steel box, contains a reading stage, pinup boards, computers, tables, chairs, and additional storage space for teaching materials.

//

Empty Nest

Newton, Mass., 2001–05

area: 460 sq. ft.

team: Jared Della Valle, Andrew Bernheimer, Erik Helgen,
    and Adam Ruedig

contractor: Ralph Gentile

The clients (creatures of habit) desired as little disruption to their living patterns as possible. This was the genesis of both the volumetric and planning strategies. By extruding the existing house twelve feet, the massing strategy allowed for immediate replication of the client's day-to-day movements through the residence. This was comforting for the client and was the single most important design criterion. Formally, the new addition is a simple extrusion of the Colonial house and a continuation of a familiar surburban form. To differentiate the new from the old, we clad the structure in zinc-coated copper, a material used locally for roofing and flashing. As such, it lends itself to a global installation, as it is primarily used as a barrier for moisture protection. The building is wrapped very tightly, in aesthetic terms, and the zinc clings to the roof, eaves, and exterior walls. Applied in panels measuring eighteen by thirty-six inches, the zinc mimics the shingling of the existing home and the vernacular aesthetic of the neighborhood.

///

Aquacenter

Aalborg, Denmark, 2001, (pp. 134–147)

competition entry

area: 110,000 sq. ft.

team: Jared Della Valle, Andrew Bernheimer, George Dawes, and
    Ryan Harasimowicz

Our proposal for the Aquacenter in Aalborg, Denmark, presents an image of fantasy—the vision of people walking on water while others puncture and possess that same transmutable volume.

Loft

New York, N.Y., 2001

area: 4,500 sq. ft.

team: Jared Della Valle, Andrew Bernheimer, Erik Helgen, and
    Adam Ruedig

Thin-gauge wire, wrapping a metal structure, defines a bedroom and bathroom suite in a large, open loft space.

///

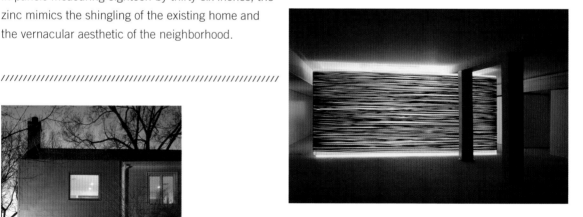

Queens Museum of Art Competition

Queens, N.Y., 2001

area: 125,000 sq. ft.
team: Jared Della Valle and Andrew Bernheimer

Our scheme for the redesign of the Queens Museum of Art involved refilling the great atrium with a new object—the Periscope of the City of New York. In an act of urban inversion, the periscope affords a sweeping view of the city upon entry to the museum and, strangely, at ground level, too. Its volume contains additional museum facilities, including administrative and curatorial offices, a library, and an education center.

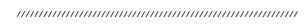

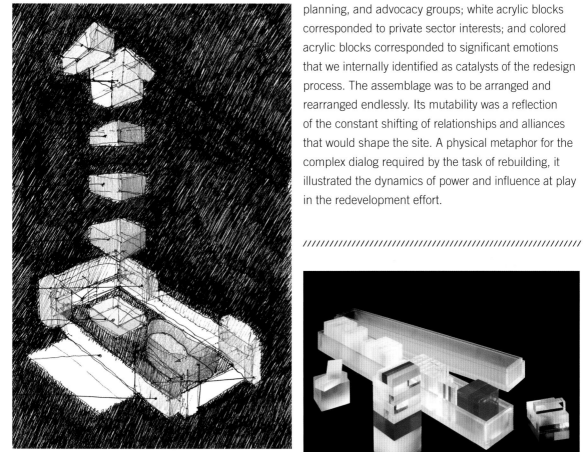

A New World Trade Center

Max Protetch Galley, New York, N.Y., 2002

team: Jared Della Valle, Andrew Bernheimer, and Aaron Levy

Our project, fabricated in advance of any concrete design proposal for the World Trade Center site, proposed neither a final program nor the finished form of any building scheme. Instead, it was a device for the study of indeterminate relationships. We identified eighty groups that declared a stake in helping shape the new downtown. To these groups, we assigned a volumetric value based on our perception of their influence on the future of the project. A block, built in scale to this assigned value and colored or textured based on interest groups, represented each entity: frosted acrylic blocks corresponded to public sector entities; clear acrylic blocks corresponded to design, planning, and advocacy groups; white acrylic blocks corresponded to private sector interests; and colored acrylic blocks corresponded to significant emotions that we internally identified as catalysts of the redesign process. The assemblage was to be arranged and rearranged endlessly. Its mutability was a reflection of the constant shifting of relationships and alliances that would shape the site. A physical metaphor for the complex dialog required by the task of rebuilding, it illustrated the dynamics of power and influence at play in the redevelopment effort.

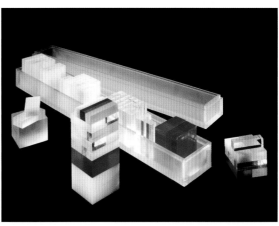

Glenmore Gardens

East New York, N.Y., 2002–07, (pp. 160–171)

area: 21,000 sq. ft.
collaborating architects: Architecture Research Office,
    BriggsKnowles Architecture + Design, and Lewis.Tsurumaki.Lewis
team: Jared Della Valle, Andrew Bernheimer, Erik Helgen,
    Adam Ruedig, and Brian Butterfield
developers: Just Green LLC, ET Partners (Richard Eaddy and
    Phil Tugendrajch) with CPC Resources and Della Valle
    Bernheimer Development
contractor: Triple Crown Contracting, Michael Cassino, and
    Joe Fedelim, partners

In collaboration with three other architecture firms, DB
designed and developed ten affordable houses as part
of New York City's New Foundations plan.

ID/Print Magazine Offices

New York, N.Y., 2003

team: Jared Della Valle, Andrew Bernheimer, and Erik Helgen

///

Hoboken 9-11 Memorial

Hoboken, N.J., 2003

team: Jared Della Valle, Andrew Bernheimer, and Adam Ruedig
landscape architect: Thomas Balsley Associates (Steven Tupu)

Like a field of flowers, scores of tiny video
screens display glowing landscapes and portraits,
memorializing the events and aftermath of September
11. These images show, in real time, the renaissance
and regrowth of the places attacked on that day, as
well as recorded eulogies to those who were lost in the
tragedy. The design displaces visitors to distant places
and offers them the chance to witness the progress
of time and the healing of physical, emotional, and
national wounds, and to meet people they otherwise
would never have known.

///

Media Kiosk for Creative Time

New York, N.Y., 2003

team: Jared Della Valle, Andrew Bernheimer, and Adam Ruedig

Hundreds of orange balls—emblazoned with the Creative Time logo and containing a piece of paper with curatorial information and a map locating Art Cluster installations—bounce inside a thirty-foot-long vitrine in the center of Duffy Square. Visitors to the square may reach within the vitrine to grab one of the balls for themselves, to take with them in their search for public art. Their initial participation in this "information grab" results in a happening: a group dance recital, a twisting crowd of people reaching for the balls, on display for all to see in the kinetic atmosphere of Times Square.

//

Loft

New York, N.Y., 2003–05

area: 5,000 sq. ft.

team: Jared Della Valle, Andrew Bernheimer, Erik Helgen, and
    Brian Butterfield

A box fabricated from metal bar grating, typically used for sidewalk installations, delineates spaces in a vast urban loft.

Private Residence

Fire Island, N.Y., 2004–06

area: 1,600 sq. ft.

team: Jared Della Valle, Andrew Bernheimer, and Suzanne Stefan

The architecture of this house endeavors to blur the distinction between inside and outside through the use of deeply cantilevering volumes and planes. These shapes simultaneously shelter the occupants from the sun, draw the eye to the outside by framing views of the Atlantic Ocean, and bring the inhabitants to the territory outside the house.

//

Artreehoose

New Fairfield, Conn., 2004–08, (pp.64–77)

team: Jared Della Valle, Andrew Bernheimer, Erik Helgen,
    Brian Butterfield, and Suzanne Stefan
structural engineer: Guy Nordenson Associates Structural
    Engineers, Guy Nordenson and Brett Schneider
contractor: Hammersmith, Inc

Taking cues from the surrounding landscape, this
house floats and protects the adjacent ground, much
like the trees on the site.

23 Beekman Place

New York, N.Y., 2004–06, (pp.92–107)

team: Jared Della Valle, Andrew Bernheimer, Adam Ruedig,
    Burck Schellenberg, Brian Butterfield, Kari Anderson, and
    Gregory Horgan
contractor: CW Contracting, Corey Ward

A renovation, restoration, and intervention of Paul
Rudolph's former apartment on Manhattan's East Side.

Butterfly Pavilion

Tulsa, Okla., 2004–05, (pp.54–63)

team: Jared Della Valle, Andrew Bernheimer, Burck Schellenberg,
    Suzanne Stefan, and Brian Butterfield

This design for a garden structure made from laser-cut
steel, for the Philbrook Museum of Art, finds its origins
in the spirit and etymology of the word *pavilion*, derived
from the Latin *papilion*, meaning butterfly.

///

801 Chestnut Street

Philadelphia, Penn., 2005

area: 730,000 sq. ft.
team: Jared Della Valle, Andrew Bernheimer, Burck Schellenberg,
    Adam Ruedig, and Brian Butterfield

Irregularly deployed stone piers create a modulated
facade in this tall mixed-use structure.

///

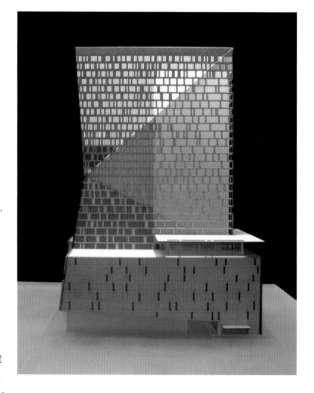

245 Tenth

New York, N.Y., 2005–08, (pp. 22–37)

team: Jared Della Valle, Andrew Bernheimer, Garrick Jones,
    Erik Helgen, Burck Schellenberg, and Andrew Willard
client: Grasso Holdings, Philadelphia, Penn.
architect of record: Goshow Architects
contractor: J. Petrocelli
structural engineer: Robert Silman Associates, Nat Oppenheimer
MEP: Robert Derector Associates, Isaac Vanunu
civil engineer: Langan, Alan Poeppel
facade consultant: FRONT, Mike Ra

This 54,000-square-foot residential condominium in
the Chelsea arts district uses images derived from the
steam trains that previously rode along the adjacent
High Line tracks as a derivation for form and surface.

Copper House

2005–07, Columbia County, N.Y. (pp.78–91)

team: Jared Della Valle, Andrew Bernheimer, Erik Helgen, and
    Brian Butterfield
contractor: Dean Builders

Built as a weekend home for a family of four, this
house was conceived as a time-tracking device for
registering day-to-day environmental changes and for
measuring the transformations of a nuclear family over
months, years, and decades.

///

Private Residence

Westhampton, N.Y., 2006

area: 1,600 sq. ft.
team: Jared Della Valle, Andrew Bernheimer, Garrick Jones, and
    Andrew Willard

This 1,800-square-foot beach house is the prototype
undertaking for a prefab home design, to be
manufactured and marketed as a modestly sized
and priced, environmentally friendly "eco-retreat" in
a variety of configurations. The house is conceived
as a series of formally articulated, programmatically
conflated prefabricated units, which are occupied
alternately, blurring the line between outside and inside
spaces but also delineating a program of excursion
and retreat. The house is simultaneously open to its
surroundings and able to withstand severe weather.
The first floor of the house is inhabited around a
series of intensely compact programmatic elements of
kitchen, living room, and stair. The walls between these
elements are made of a series of retractable glass
doors, allowing most of the floor to open out onto the
surrounding decks and landscape.

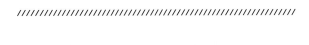

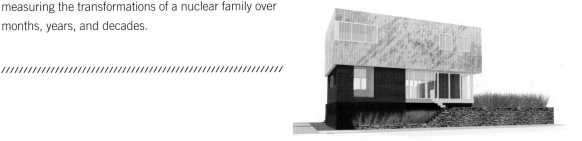

459 West 18th

New York, N.Y., 2006–08, (pp. 38–53)

area: 34,000 sq. ft.

team: Jared Della Valle, Andrew Bernheimer, Garrick Jones, Erik Helgen, Burck Schellenberg, Adam Ruedig, Andrew Willard, A. J. Pires, and Cathy Braasch
client: Della Valle Bernheimer Development
contractor: TG Nickel and Associates
structural engineer: Robert Silman Associates, Nat Oppenheimer
civil engineer: Langan, Alan Poeppel
facade consultant: FRONT, Mike Ra

Two interlocking volumes, one in black and one in white, reveal the zoning requirements of the site in this residential condominium development.

Stockholm Public Library Competition

2006

team: Jared Della Valle, Andrew Bernheimer, Burck Schellenberg, Erik Helgen, A. J. Pires, Cathy Braasch, Javier Santamaria, and Dylan Sauer

Inspired by the deposits of rock left by the slowly receding glaciers that shaped the topography of Stockholm, our extension to Erik Gunnar Asplund's Stockholm Public Library provides sheltered book collections bordering on luminous interior public spaces and newly formed plazas. Drawing inspiration from the neighboring esker and its geological formation, the deposits of the library's collections are exposed to the public as opaque, monumental boxes embedded in the vertical mass of the new extension. A large hole cut through the extension allows light and views between the street and hill, bringing the energy of street traffic to the inner territory of the hillside plaza and further emphasizing the connection between library and landscape. The involvement of Stockholm's glass craftsmen is a vital element of the construction

of the new library. The design incorporates an exterior enclosure of panels punctured by glass lenses, drawn from the form of Asplund's original iconic building. During the day, these glass lenses will transform and magnify light. Visitors passing through the library will have constant yet varied views of the surrounding city. At night, these lenses will act like candles, creating a beacon within the city and casting diffuse and refracted light onto the plazas surrounding the libraries, reinforcing the vibrancy of this important public space.

//

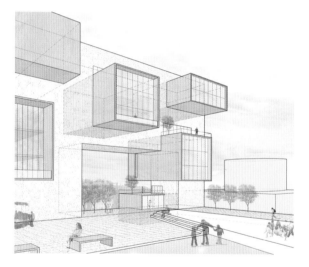

//

Zinc House

Fire Island, N.Y., 2006

team: Jared Della Valle, Andrew Bernheimer, and Brian Butterfield
contractor: BroCon

A recladding of a severely deteriorated house, this project served as a laboratory for modern, sustainable, and weather-resistant materials.

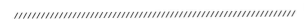

JACK Table

patent pending, 2006–07

team: Jared Della Valle, Andrew Bernheimer, Kari Anderson, and
　Adam Ruedig

A reinvention of the common work table, JACK was created to address the various ergonomic, technological, and aesthetic requirements of everyday work surfaces in an economical fashion. Its name arose from its resemblance to a familiar toy, a lighthearted reference to the flexibility and skill involved in the children's game of the same name.

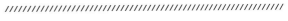

Splash!

2006–07

project team: Jared Della Valle, Andrew Bernheimer, Garrick Jones,
    and Andrew Willard

Designed for RIFRA Milano, translucent vessels reveal splashes of color hidden within bathroom cabinetry.

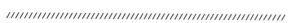

Maine State Pier

Portland, Maine, 2007

area: 200,000 sq. ft.

team: Jared Della Valle, Andrew Bernheimer, Garrick Jones,
    Burck Schellenberg, Cathy Braasch, Andrew Willard, and
    Brian Butterfield

This scheme proposes a 150,000-square-foot redevelopment of Portland's currently dilapidated Maine State Pier, as a large-scale, multimodal business and leisure destination. The pier is situated at the cusp between Portland's existing commercial waterfront district and the recently rezoned industrial eastern waterfront. The project creates new pier infrastructure that floats twenty-five feet aboveground and runs the length of the existing pier, sloping down to meet the at-grade park at an access point to the city. Below this raised pier is nestled a series of glass and wood boxes with small vertical, stainless-steel structural fins. These contain restaurants and cafes, a local fish and farmer's cooperative, and marine uses for a multitude of berthing and industrial capacities.

Bryce Wolkowitz Gallery

New York, N.Y., 2007–08

area: 2,000 sq. ft.

team: Jared Della Valle, Andrew Bernheimer, Erik Helgen,
   Burck Schellenberg, and Sarah Ingham

A gallery for artists who work in diverse digital media, this series of three distinct zones is articulated by a single mute box that spans the width of the space.

Soho Hotel

New York, N.Y., 2007–10

area: 100,000 sq. ft.

team: Jared Della Valle, Andrew Bernheimer, Garrick Jones,
   Burck Schellenberg, Andrew Willard, Cathy Braasch,
   Sarah Ingham, and Janine Soper

client: Integrated Development

structural engineer: Robert Silman Associates

civil engineer: Mueser Rutledge

facade consultant: FRONT, Mike Ra

///

Lightbox House

East Hampton, N.Y., 2007–09

area: 3,300 sq. ft.

team: Jared Della Valle, Andrew Bernheimer, Garrick Jones,
   Lara Shihab-Eldin, Andrew Willard, and Brian Butterfield

A house for two photographers is described as two boxes of cedar and concrete. An irregular pattern of windows is composed to highlight specific moments in the landscape surrounding the house.

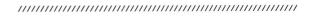

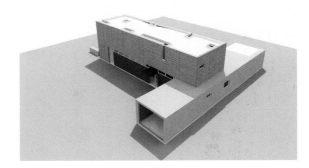

Hudson Yards: Migration

New York, N.Y., 2007–08 (pp. 110–121)

scheme 1: 500,000 sq. ft.

collaborator: Architecture Research Office (ARO)

DB team: Jared Della Valle, Andrew Bernheimer, Erik Helgen,
Burck Schellenberg, Maxwell Worrell, Lara Shihab-Eldin,
Cathy Braasch, A. J. Pires, Brian Butterfield, Matthew Nowaczyk,
Jonathan Gonzalez

ARO team: Stephen Cassell, Adam Yarinsky, Michael Regan,
Jeffrey Hong, and Jane Lea

structural engineer: Guy Nordenson and Associates Structural
Engineers, Guy Nordenson and Brett Schneider

facade consultant: FRONT

client: Alloy Development

This building reinvents urban views through the manipulation of reflections. Facets or folds within a modular facade create fractured views. Shearing conditions connect the disconnected: the sky and the street, north and south, front and back, top and bottom. The collection of units makes a larger mark in the city.

Hudson Yards: Shifting

New York, N.Y., 2007–08 (pp. 122–147)

scheme 2: approximately 1,000,000 sq. ft.

collaborator: Architecture Research Office (ARO)

DB team: Jared Della Valle, Andrew Bernheimer, Erik Helgen,
Maxwell Worrell, A. J. Pires, and Matthew Nowaczyk

ARO team: Stephen Cassell, Adam Yarinsky, Jeffrey Hong, and Jane Lea

client: Alloy Development

The formation of the tower—a playful interpretation of zoning requirements—reiterates the stepping planes of rooftops and forms an abstracted and compressed interpretation of the Manhattan skyline. The required setback shifts over the face of the building, resulting in unexpected view corridors and areas of outdoor space. Differences in reflectivity, along with the shifting of mullions from inside to outside of the glass, modulate the facade and cause a visual inversion, effectively doubling the perception of the shift.

Think/Make Exhibition

Syracuse University School of Architecture, 2008

team: Jared Della Valle, Andrew Bernheimer, Garrick Jones, Janine Soper, and Brian Butterfield

A series of translucent displays—attached to an armature of aluminum components—double as graphic information about the firm and a light source for viewing project models.

///

///

R-House

Winning entry, From the Ground Up, competition

Syracuse, N.Y. 2008–09

collaborator: Architecture Research Office (ARO)

area: 1200 sq. ft.

team: DB: Andrew Bernheimer, Jared Della Valle, Garrick Jones,
Lara Shihab-Eldin, Janine Soper; ARO: Adam Yarinsky and
Stephen Cassell, partners, Megumi Tamonaha, Jane Lea, Neil Patel,
and Melissa Eckerman

consultants: Transsolar, Guy Nordenson Associates, Stuart-Lynn
Companies, Coen+Partners

R-House presents an affordable, innovative paradigm for minimal energy consumption embodied in architecture that nurtures the spirit and engages the community. Framed within its iconic exterior are expansive and luminous spaces that require only the equivalent energy of a hair dryer for heating.

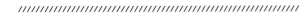

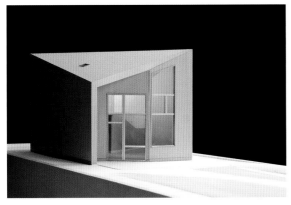

HR&A Advisors

New York, N.Y., 2008

area: 8,000 sq. ft.

team: Jared Della Valle, Andrew Bernheimer, Erik Helgen, Max Worrell

contractor: McGovern

Soft boundaries buffer sound and create pockets of intimate spaces within a large downtown loft.

Loft Residences

Brooklyn, N.Y., 2008–09

area: 105,000 sq. ft.

team: Jared Della Valle, Andrew Bernheimer, Erik Helgen,
Burck Schellenberg, Max Worrell, Andrew Willard, Sarah Ingham,
Kate Patterson, Jonathan Gonzalez

A single city block is broken down in scale by two elements containing large loft residences. These two blocks are carved away, bringing green space into surprising locations within the buildings.

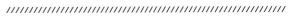

Awards

Dwell Nice Modernist Award, 2007

AIA Special Citation for Innovative Design for Affordable Housing, Glenmore Gardens, 2007

Emerging Voices Award, Architectural League of New York, 2007

AIA Honor Award for Interior Architecture, 23 Beekman Place, 2007

LANDed Garden Pavilion Competition, Philbrook Museum of Art, Tulsa, Okla., 2005

Distinguished Alumni Award, Washington University, St. Louis, Mo., 2003

Young Architects Forum, Architectural League of New York, 2002

AIA Staten Island Citation, P. S. 18/L!brary, 2002

GSA Design Awards Landscape Citation, 450 Golden Gate Plaza, 2000

ID Annual Design Review Honorable Mention: Environments, 450 Golden Gate Plaza, 2000

San Francisco Prize, 1st Place, for Building Intimacy: 450 Golden Gate Plaza Competition, 1996

///

Exhibitions

InSightUSA, Aedes Architectural Forum in Berlin, Germany, 2008

Think/Make, Syracuse University School of Architecture in Syracuse, N.Y., 2008

44 Young Architects, SCALAE in Santiago de Compostela, Spain, 2007

Young Americans: New Architecture in the USA, Deutsches Architekturmuseum in Frankfurt, Germany, 2007

New New York: Fast Forward, Architectural League of New York, New York, N.Y., 2007

LANDed Garden Pavilion, Philbrook Museum of Art, Tulsa, Okla., 2005

New York 3: Small Civic Projects, Architectural League of New York, New York, N.Y., 2002

A New World Trade Center, Venice Architecture Biennale, Venice, Italy, 2002

Young Architects Forum: Material Process, Architectural League of New York, New York, N.Y., 2002

A New World Trade Center, National Building Museum, Washington, D.C., 2002

A New World Trade Center, Max Protetch Gallery, New York, N.Y., 2002

Physical Fitness of Cities, 2002 Winter Olympic Games, Salt Lake City, Utah, 2002

Federal Design Now!, National Building Museum, Washington, D.C., 2001

Tkts 2K Competition, Van Alen Institute, New York, N.Y., 2000

Della Valle Bernheimer: Current Work, Washington University School of Architecture, St. Louis, Mo., 1999

Centering the Civic, SFMOMA, San Francisco, Calif., 1997

Diversion/Reiteration, Museo Marítim de Barcelona, Barcelona, Spain, 1996

//

Lectures

Keynote speaker, InSight USA, Aedes Architecture Forum, Berlin, Germany, 2008

Developing…, Syracuse University School of Architecture, Syracuse, N.Y., 2008

Design with a Conscience: Public Housing, The New School, New York, N.Y., 2007

New New York: High Line Forum, Architectural League of New York, New York, 2007

Emerging Voices, Architectural League of New York, New York, N.Y., 2007

Women's Committee Lecture Series on Public Space, Reed College, Portland, Oreg., 2003

Lecture Series at Cornell University School of Architecture, Ithaca, N.Y., 2003

Visiting Lecture Series at Virginia Tech, Blacksburg, Va., 2002

Young Architects Forum, Architectural League of New York, New York, N.Y., 2002

Lunch Lecture Series at the Rhode Island School of Design, Providence, R.I., 2001

Monday Night Lecture Series at Washington University, St. Louis, Mo., 1999

Young Designers Series at the Van Alen Institute, New York, N.Y., 1998

//

Selected Publications

Architectural League of New York. *Young Architects_4: Material Process.* New York: Princeton Architectural Press, 2003.

Bradbury, Dominic. "Precious Metal." *Grand Designs*, November 2008, 107–14.

Canizares, Ana G. *500 Solutions for Working at Home.* New York: Universe Publications, 2003.

Cannell, Michael. "Brooklyn Renaissance." *Dwell,* November 2007, 98–100 and 102.

Casselman, Ben. "High Design for Low-Income Housing." *The Wall Street Journal*, December 28, 2007.

"Centering the Civic: GSA Breaks New Ground." *Competitions*, Winter 1996/97, 4–15.

"Centering the Civic: The 1996 San Francisco Prize." *SFMOMA News*, March/April 1997, 6.

"Completed Competition Projects Tell the Story." *Competitions*, Spring 2000, 2–3.

Cortese, Amy. "Taking a Stroll Along the High Line." *The New York Times*, November 30, 2008.

Cutler, Steve. "Turning a Sketch into a Reality." *The Real Deal*, April 2008, 34.

"Design Review 2000." *ID Magazine*, July/August 2000, 155.

Farrelly, Liz. *Brooklyn: New Style.* New York: Thames and Hudson, 2004.

Findley, Lisa. "Urban Geography." *Architecture,* June 2000, 97–103.

Fredrickson, Eric. "Reading Room." *Architecture,* July 2002, 66–9.

Galindo, Michelle. *1000x Architecture of the Americas.* Berlin: Verlaughaus Braun, 2008.

Gregory, Rob. "Spare Change." The Architectural Review. January 2009, 82–3.

Guiney, Anne. "Green Goes the Neighborhood." *The Architect's Newspaper.* January 26, 2009.

Guiney, Anne. "Power Grid." *The Architect's Newspaper*, July 26, 2006.

Hay, David. "The Beautiful Headache." *New York Magazine*, October 2006, 52–7.

Hughes, C.J. "A Shining Moment for Builders." *The New York Times,* April 22, 2007.

Lanks, Belinda. "It's Got Legs." *Metropolis*, June 2007, 140–1.

Lieberman, Paul. "One Small Footprint and One Giant Leap." *The Los Angeles Times*, March 5, 2008.

Louie, Elaine. "HOUSE PROUD; Privacy? In a Loft? Wide Open Spaces Face Subdivision." *The New York Times*, June 3, 1999.

Manfra, Laurie. "Issue 11: Modern Adaptations." *Materials Monthly,* September 2007, 4–11.

Max Protetch Gallery. *A New World Trade Center.* Los Angeles: ReganBooks, 2002.

Millard, Bill. "High Ideals, Low Budget." *Oculus* 69, no. 3 (Fall 2007): 26–8.

Nobel, Philip. "Top Ten." *Artforum*, December 2002, 122–3.

Nobel, Philip. *Sixteen Acres.* New York: Metropolitan Books, 2005.

Nyren, Ron. "Very First Federal." *Metropolis*, February/March 1999, 44 and 46.

Pietro, Silvia. "San Francisco Federal Plaza." *Abitare* 407 (June 2001): 50–51.

Sheftell, Jason. "Young Blood." *New York Daily News,* March 30, 2007.

Shnier, Kohn. "More for Less." *Azure,* September 2007, 122–5.

Credits

Sokol, David. "Housing Slump? What Housing Slump?" *Business Week*, January 4, 2008.

Sommerhoff, Emilie. "Home Turf." *Architecture*, August 2003, 73–4.

Stephens, Suzanne. "Paul Rudolph's Penthouse." *Architectural Record*, June 2007, 116–21 and 230.

Thomas, Kelly Devine. "Filling a Void." *ARTnews,* April 2002, 122.

Urbach, Henry. "Full Metal Jacket." *Interior Design*, August 2001, 236–9.

Zacks, Stephen. "The Affordable Housing Complex." *Metropolis*, October 2008, 128–31 and 170–1.

///

Front Matter
pp. 11, 13 bottom left, 17 right, Richard Barnes; p. 14 far right, Peter Mauss/ESTO, all others Richard Barnes; p. 15 left two, Frank Oudeman, second from right, Encore; p. 19, *Close Encounters of the Third Kind*, 1977, renewed in 2005 by Columbia Pictures Industries, Inc.; all others, Della Valle Bernheimer.

245 Tenth
p. 22 left, courtesy Charles & Clint; pp. 23, 33, 34 top, and 37, Frank Oudeman; pp. 30–1: BLiP; pp. 32 and 34 bottom, Encore; all others, Della Valle Bernheimer.

459 West 18th
pp. 39 and 51, BLiP; pp. 41, 42–3, 49, 50, and 52–3, Frank Oudeman; all others, Della Valle Bernheimer.

Butterfly Pavilion
All images by Della Valle Bernheimer.

Artreehoose
pp. 64 right, 65, 71, 72, 74, 75, and 76–7, Richard Barnes; p. 69 courtesy Guy Nordenson Associates; all others, Della Valle Bernheimer.

Copper House
pp. 79, 81, 83, 84, 85 top left and right, 87, 88–9, 90 top, and 91, Richard Barnes; all others, Della Valle Bernheimer.

23 Beekman Place
pp. 92 right, 93, 98 center two, 99, 100, 101, 103, 104 all except top left, 106, and 107, Richard Barnes; pp. 94 right and 95 right, Peter Aaron/ESTO; all others, Della Valle Bernheimer.

Hudson Yards: Migration
p. 110 left most, Richard Barnes; pp. 111 and 115, Encore; p. 119, courtesy Guy Nordenson Associates; all others, Della Valle Bernheimer.

Hudson Yards: Shifting
pp. 123, 125, 130, 131, and 132–3, Encore; all others, Della Valle Bernheimer.

Aquacenter
All images by Della Valle Bernheimer.

450 Golden Gate Plaza
pp. 149, 151 bottom, 152–3, 155, Richard Barnes; all others, Della Valle Bernheimer.

Glenmore Gardens
pp. 161, 165 bottom, 166 bottom, 167 bottom, 168, 170–71, 173 far left, Richard Barnes; p. 162 top left, courtesy ARO, bottom left, courtesy Lewis.Tsurumaki.Lewis, bottom right, courtesy BriggsKnowles Architecture and Design; all others, Della Valle Bernheimer.

Project Index
pp. 174 top right, 175, and 179 right, Peter Mauss/ESTO; p. 176 far left, Richard Barnes; p. 177 far right, Jock Pottle; p. 178 left, courtesy *ID* magazine; p. 184 top and bottom left, Encore; all others, Della Valle Bernheimer.

///